Lessons FROM HORSES

Randy Helm

ISBN 978-1-64191-872-5 (paperback)
ISBN 978-1-64191-873-2 (digital)

Christian Faith Publishing, Inc.
832 Park Avenue
Meadville, PA 16335
www.christianfaithpublishing.com

Printed in the United States of America

Contents

· ·

Horses have a lot to teach us if we are able to recognize the lessons.

For me, the opportunity presented itself at a point in life when I didn't expect it and at a time when I definitely didn't want to be taught anything.

Life seemed to have turned upside down, and without realizing it, I had pushed aside the feelings of disappointment by focusing on horses and horse training.

I wasn't angry with God. I was just numb. It was early one morning. I was working a young mare for the first time in the round pen. For whatever reason, she wouldn't move beyond running around in circles. She would go clockwise, counterclockwise, and turn inside toward me. However, she seemed unable to grasp the concept and cues to simply stop, face me, and rest. I continued trying everything I knew to get her to relax, but she continued at an anxious trot. After about thirty minutes, I said, "If you would just stop and face me, things would be so much better." It that moment I felt something of a whisper, "Randy, if you would just stop running and face me, things would be so much better." Suddenly in that moment, I recognized the teacher was this young horse and I was the student.

Chapter 1

The Round Pen

The word which came to Jeremiah from the LORD, saying: "Arise and go down to the potter's house, and there I will cause you to hear My words." Then I went down to the potter's house, and there he was, making something at the wheel.
                    —Jeremiah 18:1–2 (NKJV)

Imagine in forty-five minutes, your ordinary life being radically changed as you learn to yield the direction you are moving, recognize what to turn away from and toward, understand what produces peace, and learn how to rest.

I don't know of anyone who would expect to learn this much in months, yet the average horse begins to comprehend this in about forty-five minutes in the round pen.

The round pen is where the foundation begins for horses and the parallels to life are abundant.

Horse training and spiritual growth must begin somewhere. In training horses, it generally begins in a round pen. Spiritual growth and life itself have a lot of parallels to the horse round pen if we will only recognize them. Too often we miss the lessons and get frustrated with the process.

Somewhere around 1990, I purchased a VHS tape series by John Lyons called *Round Pen Reasoning*, and it changed my entire approach to understanding and training horses.

The round pen allows the horse to move in circles around the trainer and provides a safe environment for the horse to learn. It is that place where movement into a new life begins for the horse and where a foundation for training is formed. The movement around the trainer starts a process of interaction that develops a basic language that will continue for the life of the horse and trainer.

The one word I want to be able to communicate is *yes*. Every time the horse gets it right, I remove as much pressure as I can, and eventually that becomes my yes. When the pressure goes away, he understands he did something right, which allows him to relax. I think of it as providing an atmosphere of peace, and eventually a life once dominated by fear is gradually transformed and replaced with peace.

In many respects, horses and people have a lot in common. Horses don't like pressure and discomfort, so they avoid it if at all possible. When the pressure is gone, the horse experiences peace. I have worked with hundreds of horses and thousands of people, and I am convinced we are all essentially looking for the same thing.

Peace doesn't come automatically in training or in life. As a matter of fact, most training begins with pressure and movement, allowing the trainer to find opportunities to say yes.

The round pen is designed for movement, and there is no room for apathy or indifference. When I walk into the round pen, I expect the horse to do something. It is almost impossible to work with an indifferent horse, and it is almost impossible to work with an indifferent person.

As the horse trots in circles around me, I ask the horse to change directions until the horse turns toward me (inside turns). Once the horse turns toward me, I remove the pressure by relaxing my body and taking a half step back. After a while, the horse figures out that turning toward me is less stressful, and eventually he will stop and face me. When that happens, all the pressure goes away, and the horse rests (no pressure equals peace and becomes my way of saying yes).

It is essential that the horse moves in response to the trainer's cues. Without movement, the horse cannot learn. Once the horse begins to move, training can begin. People often have the same problem. For us to change, we need to do something. If we are waiting to be different or better without doing something, we will never arrive.

An old Farmall tractor taught me a great lesson on the importance of movement. At the age of about nine, I was expected to drive the tractor on the farm. I soon learned that it took all the strength I had to simply turn the steering wheel. However, once the tractor began moving, steering was pretty simple. Changing directions requires movement. Do something, or you will end up doing nothing.

Lessons from the Round Pen

Learn to Yield

In the round pen, the horse learns to yield to pressure. Often, it is one small incremental change. Put enough small changes together, and eventually the whole horse will change.

Wouldn't it be amazing if at the end of each day we simply had one thing that was better?

Surrender Direction

At first, I am not overly concerned about inside or outside turns. I simply want the horse to learn to yield direction and understand that he is not going to be hurt.

Just about every person has felt as though they were going around in circles. We are not as trainable as horses, and unfortunately, the vast majority of people fail to learn anything. Instead of learning,we either give up or speed up. What a difference could be made if we would simply let God choose the direction of our lives?

Make Mistakes and Experience Grace to Change

Grace is defined as "free and unmerited favor." That is exactly what the round pen has to be filled with. If trainers focus on the mistakes, they end up with anxious, defeated horses.

As the horse is figuring out what I want him to do, I have to remember that there will be very few big successes. Instead, there will be hundreds of small ones, which gives me hundreds of opportunities to practice my yes.

If we were keeping track of mistakes, we would become disappointed and eventually overwhelmed, because in the beginning, the mistakes always outnumber the successes. Mistakes are part of the process. I prefer to see the round pen not as a place where mistakes are made but where learning occurs. As a trainer, I am focused on giving the horse grace to help him figure out what is expected.

God understands that about us. Contrary to what many people think about God, his focus is always on when we get it right.

Job 14:16 says, "*For now You number my steps, You do not observe my sins.*"

8

I love this scripture because it reminds us that God is aware of every step we take but does not keep track of our sins. Even though he knows every mistake we make, he looks for the times we get it right. He is waiting for us to give him the opportunity to emphatically say yes and pour out his peace.

Renew the Mind

The round pen is not a place where the horse learns to run in circles but rather a place where the horse learns to think differently. It is where the mind begins a process of transformation.

In the round pen, the horse is able to figure things out and recognize that he can make choices. It is where the horse begins to change from wild to willing.

For us, life's round pen is that place where God gives us grace as we learn how to respond to Him and figure out the right answer.

Our round pen is that place where we recognize that rather than running in circles, we can seize the opportunity to experience renewal and choose to surrender to his amazing grace.

Learn to Respond to Peace

Pressure increases stress and anxiety. Physically and emotionally, horses (and people) look for opportunities to remove themselves from pressure.

Every time the horse turns toward me, the pressure goes away. The closer the horse gets to me, the less pressure he experiences. After a while, he figures out that life in the round pen is much better when he is close, and soon many horses will refuse to leave the trainers side.

For us, life's round pen is a place where we learn peace. We run in circles thinking we are achieving success, avoiding difficulty, or getting away from God when in reality we are just wearing ourselves out.

After a while, like a horse, we begin to realize peace is much better than running, and the closer we get to God, the more peace we experience.

I am convinced the horse does not understand why there is peace, but he definitely begins to pursue it.

Learn to Stand

Having done all to stand, stand (Ephesians 6:13).

I spend quite a bit of time in the round pen teaching the horse to simply stand.

Standing is underrated in life and horse training. Too often we think we need to be doing something rather than standing still so that we can recognize what we need to do.

Movement actually teaches a horse to stand. When he moves away, he finds he has to move more, and eventually he will stand.

I have never moved away from God without having to move more than I wanted and getting worn out in the process.

A horse standing, waiting for direction, will accomplish much more than a horse prancing and spinning around. Both can have the same energy one is just in a position to use it effectively.

Like the horse, you and I need to learn to stand. Running will not only wear us out but it will also keep us from recognizing the cue to do something productive.

> *For God is working in you, giving you the desire and the power to do what pleases him.* (Philippians 2:13, NLT)

Chapter 2

Kingdoms in Conflict

Therefore, if anyone is in Christ, he is a new creature; the old things passed away; behold, new things have come.

—2 Corinthians 5:17

My first wild horse was a five-year-old dark-brown mare recently gathered from Nevada, and I named her Hershey. She soon began teaching me impromptu lessons on what it meant to be a wild horse. She was ready for flight or a fight. Her kingdom had equipped her to run away from danger, and if she couldn't run, she must fight.

Wild horses live in herds and small bands for security, companionship, and protection. Their very survival depends on a finely tuned organization of rules and systems with very specific laws that govern behavior. It is much more complex than mere survival. Wild horse herds have a lead mare that must be followed, a lead stallion that demands submission, a hierarchy that must be respected, and constant communication that is almost undetectable by human observers. These herds and bands of horses have developed a kingdom with a king, a queen, and a government.

For my life personally, the last two decades have involved a never-ending quest to understand their world and find a way to speak their language. In my opinion, discovering a way to communicate with wild horses by understanding their kingdom is really the key to success.

The first time a tried to get close to Hershey, I found myself dodging out of the way as her front hooves barely missed my outstretched arm. She then quickly spun around and tried to kick me with her back feet. I remember thinking, "What in the world have I gotten myself in to?" She was out of her element. There was no lead stallion, lead mare, or family band, and she was scared to death.

I changed tactics and tried to understand her. I tried my best to learn from her, and she became a great teacher. I soon fell in love with this amazing horse.

Once I was able to get close and pet her, I realized she was pregnant. I had her less than two months when she foaled. She watched me intently as I cared for her foal, and from that moment on, she accepted me and began a new direction in life. She decided she loved people, and we were inseparable. If I went out to the pasture, she would find me and follow me everywhere. Soon, my kingdom became her kingdom. It was a gradual transition as the instinctive flight or fight was replaced by peace and purpose.

The kingdom she knew was the reason she survived in the wild, yet the kingdom she knew was in direct conflict with the kingdom she needed.

Most people don't see life in terms of kingdoms. Yet much of life is dictated by laws that keep us in bondage and rules that dictate our actions. Like wild horses, we are subject to fear and driven by impulses.

Multitudes of men and women live within the borders of an old kingdom with laws that keep them bound to fear and failure. Many people have, what they would consider to be, good reasons to be the way they are. People, like horses, need to realize that the keys for survival in one kingdom will almost always spell a life of limitations in the other.

A life filled with limitations becomes the way we are, and the way we are eventually becomes the way we have always been.

We too often expect people to accept us just like we are even though the way we are is in desperate need of change.

"That's just who I am" and "We have always done it this way" are the greatest hindrances to attaining a meaningful future. We cannot hold on to our past and move into our future at the same time.

We all have a past that is woven into the very fabric of who we are, and our past can pull us backward if we allow it to. Henry David Thoreau said, "*Never look back unless you are planning to go that way.*"

Wild horses are connected to a kingdom that contains laws that were in place before they were born and behaviors they must develop if they are going to survive.

Like Hershey, you and I must allow God to demonstrate His love for us as He graciously translates us out of a kingdom of fear and failure into a kingdom of His peace and power. Colossians 1:13 (NLT) says, "*For he has rescued us from the kingdom of darkness and transferred us into the Kingdom of his dear Son.*"

There is not a single lesson I have learned from horses that has been more impactful on my life than the lesson of kingdoms in conflict.

Horse training is full of conflict. Every horse wants me to abide by his rules and live according to his kingdom. Much like I want God to live by my rules. Just like the horse, I struggle to understand why God's plan could possibly be better than mine. To be quite honest, God's plan for my life is often the opposite of what I want to do. So like any good Christian, I include God in my life and begin taking from his world the things I think I can use in my world. I continue doing things my way believing he will understand and all the while assuming he will change.

I am not the first one to believe that God may come around to my way of thinking. In Psalms 50:21, God says, "*These things you have done, and I kept silent; You thought that I was altogether like you.*"

The Bible is filled with men and women who struggled to change from a kingdom of fear and failure to a kingdom of life. This battle between the law of the flesh and law of the Spirit is like the battle a horse has when renewing the mind and moving past the patterns and laws of the old kingdom. Romans 6 refers to our old man (the person before Christ or without Christ) as being in bondage to a destructive way of thinking and living.

In Romans Chapter 6, Paul wrote about how the laws from his former life controlled him. In Chapter 7, he goes on to say that the things he wanted to do, he didn't do, and the things he didn't want to do, he did. (Sound familiar?) The struggles for Paul and the struggles for the rest of us are resolved in Romans 8:2, "*For the law of the Spirit of life in Christ Jesus has made me free from the law of sin and death.*"

Like horses, we have to realize that the defenses that we think help us survive too often become the greatest obstacle to an amazing future and success.

If you hold on to your history you will always do it at the expense of your destiny.
—T. D. Jakes

Chapter 3

Overcoming Fear

There is no fear in love; but perfect love casts out fear, because fear involves torment. But he who fears has not been made perfect in love.

—1 John 4:18

One of the first horses I trained for the Trainer Incentive Program was a pretty little sorrel mare. She had never been touched (at least willingly) and, as expected, had a lot of fear. This mare, however, seemed to have an unusual level of anxiety. She progressed somewhat average in her training and began to comprehend what I wanted her to do. Eventually she faced me, stood still, allowed me to pet her, and soon was following me everywhere. When I rubbed or brushed her face and withers, she would relax and stand still. However, the moment I moved toward her rear, she would panic and run. I worked for hours to reassure her that I wasn't going to hurt her, and inch by inch she allowed me to move further down her body. Finally, once behind her, I was shocked to see long scars on both her sides. The scars started from her hips and ended at her back knees. Even though the wounds had healed, the scars told a story. A story that reminded this horse that pain can be unbearable and predators can be cruel. Looking at the scars, it was obvious that she had survived an attack by a mountain lion. She stood there trembling as tears began to well up in my eyes. I knew she had no idea what I was saying, but somehow I felt I needed to tell her how sorry I was that this had happened to her.

The world she was born into gave her instincts and, combined with her experiences, developed behaviors that helped her survive as a wild mustang. She possessed defenses that helped her stay alive. The laws of the old kingdom told her that too much trust or complacency could cause her pain.

Now she had an opportunity to begin an entirely new life. A new kingdom was in front of her even though she didn't know it. For her to succeed in the new kingdom, she would have to learn to move past the fear.

As her trainer, I had to remember where she came from. Each horse, whether wild or domestic, has a past. I remind myself of that with horses—and with people.

Horses and people have similar fears. Some fears are based in knowledge and experience, while others have no basis at all. The Bible tells us that "perfect love casts out fear." I have heard people define this as some sort of admonition for them to develop perfect love so they would not be afraid. There is no question that it is important that each of us grow in love, but I don't believe God is telling us that if we were to somehow develop perfect love, we would not experience fear. God is the only One with perfect love, and for us he is the only One that can cast out all fear. I believe what God wants us to know is that his perfect love will eventually destroy fear. Real fear or imagined fear, the answer is faith in God, faith in who he is, faith in what he can do, and faith that he loves us unconditionally.

We, like horses, discover that in life there are limitations and that we are not invincible. At some point, every wild horse will be faced with difficulties including injuries, drought, and predators.

Like the horse, at some point, every person will encounter tragedy, trials, and difficulty. Jesus said, *"I have told you all this so that you may have peace in me. Here on earth you will have many trials and sorrows. But take heart, because I have overcome the world"* (John 16:33, NLT).

The fear and worry associated with hardship and struggle can too easily define our lives. We all experience loss and pain, and many people become convinced that they will never be free. We see unfortunate things happen to others and live life in fear they will happen to us as well. The similarities between our new life and that of a wild horse are abundant. Like the sorrel mare, we can survive a tragedy only to be defeated by the fear that it will happen again.

If I want the horse to trust me, I must, to the best of my ability, imitate God's perfect love. My job as a trainer is to love the horses enough to help them work through their fears. I am not concerned about my horse loving me, and I have no way of knowing whether or not he does. I don't possess perfect love, but I do my best to equip the horse with tools to replace the fear with faith and confidence.

Faith and love are inseparable. Faith in God and being secure in his love constantly remind us that we can accomplish more than we dreamed and that we are greater than our self-imposed limitations. I want every horse I train to discover new opportunities and accomplish things they never dreamed possible. Love provides an opportunity for horses and people to live a brand-new life. Too often we settle for a life modified around fear rather than a life conquering fear.

We give horses a new life, providing them with food and water, shelter, and protection. Because we care for these animals, we try to provide a life free from the things they fear. If we do that for our horses, imagine how much more God will do for us. Like the wild horse, God promises us a new life, a life that is radically different from the life that we have grown accustomed to. We are promised a life that is drastically different from the life of fear and insecurity.

Overcoming fear is rarely an event. It is almost always a process.

The process of overcoming fear begins with overcoming the little things. Take a step toward what is in front of you and trust God that he will make a way. It is God who says, *"Fear not, for I am with you; Be not dismayed, for I am your God. I will strengthen you, Yes, I will help you, I will uphold you with My righteous right hand"* (Isaiah 41:10, NKJV).

In the state prison horse training facility, I am fortunate enough to have a seven-acre obstacle course filled with tires, tarps, pedestals, teetering bridges, and running water, to name few. When the horse is first introduced to these, he does not see obstacles but things that he is afraid of. To overcome fear and master these obstacles, we begin by getting the horse to take one step forward on cue. That's it, nothing too complicated, just one step. When a horse is confronted with something he is afraid of, whether small or large, the same thing is asked: one step. Before long, enough one steps becomes a journey.

Sometimes it is one step forward and ten steps backward. That is where I must demonstrate enough compassion and consistency to let the horse figure it out.

If I will do that for a horse, how much more will God patiently help us overcome those things that we fear? Your journey to overcome fear begins with one step forward knowing that God loves you enough to help you work through your fear one step at a time. Enough one steps, and before long, you and God will arrive at a place of confidence and assurance.

If you want to conquer fear, don't sit home and think about it. Go out and get busy. (Dale Carnegie)

Chapter 4

Moving Beyond the Past

Do not call to mind the former things, Or ponder things of the past. Behold, I will do something new, Now it will spring forth; Will you not be aware of it? I will even make a roadway in the wilderness, Rivers in the desert.

—Isaiah 43:18–19

An amazing horse reminded me that the past does not have to define you and abuse does not have the power to rob you of your purpose and destiny.

In the spring of 2011, I started working with a beautiful black wild mustang. The horse's life with people had not begun well. When the horse arrived at my corral, he could barely walk. All four of his feet had been hobbled with a thin rope, cutting deep wounds into the fetlocks (area above the hoof). I learned that this wild mustang had been choked down while inside a horse trailer, hobbled, and dragged out into cactus.

This horse was petrified with fear. I was furious that anyone could treat an animal like this and was concerned this horse may never become physically sound, let alone trust people.

I always start horses the same way, well *almost always*. This horse would be different.

I didn't ask him to move. Instead, I began the training process by simply and gently petting him and reassuring him that he would not be hurt.

The cactus thorns on his sides and legs were easily seen, and I knew they had to be causing a lot of pain. However, once he began to relax enough for me to touch him, I could see that cactus needles were also imbedded all over his stomach, the inside of his legs, and his groin. The challenge of removing the cactus from his legs was going to be difficult enough, but I was sure the groin area was going to be dangerous and risky. Gently but quickly, I pulled the first needle out as he jerked backward. With the removal of the second needle, he merely flinched, and by the third needle, he started to relax. There was an audible sigh of relief as I continued removing the painful needles. It was as though he realized at that moment that I was trying to help him.

The healing process of the physical and emotional wounds began, and during this time, he began teaching me lessons on overcoming the past. I soon learned that this horse had an amazing capacity to forgive and to trust.

The process of adjusting to his new life was not an easy one.

The first few times I came toward his stall, he was noticeably nervous—ears forward, muscles tense, and eyes that followed my every move. Yet over time I noticed that he was beginning to relax, and soon he would slowly limp over to meet me. I asked little from him other than to trust me. Every chance I got, I rewarded him by petting, brushing, and softly reassuring him that everything was going to be okay. I would stand beside him, place my hands on his big head, and pray that God would heal his body and heart.

Finally, I reached down to get a closer look at the deep wounds in his injured ankle, and as I did, he gently placed his big hoof in my hands. As he allowed me to hold the foot that another person had injured, I knew we were on our way to recovery.

The past is a powerful thing. If we allow it to, it can lock us in its prison with no doors out and no windows to see what the future may hold. The prison of the past constantly whispers, and sometimes screams, that things will never be better. The pain of the past can only remind of what happened. It has no power to tell us what we can become.

Human pain is much more confining than that of a horse. Like this horse as he watched me approach his pen, we watch life come at us and determine that we must protect ourselves from the possibility of pain and disappointment. Unfortunately, it is difficult for us to limp over to the possibilities in front of us and dare to hope that things can change.

This amazing horse began to allow me to bandage his wounds, and soon he was following me around the arena like a big puppy. By the time he healed, I was his undeserving hero.

The first time I rode him was in a clinic for women only. The clinic was promoted by churches, therapists, and shelters for abused women. The response was overwhelming. I shared his story and his journey to trust again. I talked about his abuse, his fear of people, and the process to healing. Then I climbed into the pen, and he immediately walked over to me and placed his big head on my shoulder. With no lead rope or halter, he followed me all over the round pen, refusing to leave my side. I put the bridle and saddle on him, reassured him he was fine, and calmly climbed on his back. He stood there relaxed, not moving a muscle. Soon he was gently carrying me all around the pen. As I continued talking about his story of overcoming abuse, I noticed that the crowd had become unusually quiet. Looking up, I saw tear-filled eyes everywhere as tissues were being passed from row to row. As I choked back my own tears, I went on to talk about the wonderful future this horse now had. A young lady was there who wanted to adopt him. She took him home that day.

I named him Phoenix because he rose from the ashes of abuse and pain.

Abuse can be paralyzing. The physical pains heal much quicker than the emotional ones. There are no Band-Aids or stitches for emotional pain. However, we can learn a lot from horses. They have this amazing ability to see things in the now. What happened yesterday has less effect on them because now things can be different. The person who is kind to them today allows them to reframe what they think about people, and somehow, they have the ability to decide that people have changed.

I wish I were more like Phoenix. Unfortunately, I have thousands of memories that I can recall. Many are good; others are not. My memories can produce the same feelings I had years, even decades ago. As a result, I can become depressed or angry over things that are far removed from today, and somehow those things can drag me backward and keep me from moving forward.

After spending years working with horses and training mustangs, I have come to the conclusion that horses don't have the ability to dwell on memories. They develop behaviors that are built on a combination of experiences without being encumbered by the motives and circumstances surrounding things in the past. Because of this, I believe they have the unique ability to replace a bad experience with a good one.

Unfortunately, you and I don't have that ability. As a matter of fact, one of our greatest hindrances to overcoming abuse is the memory or memories.

Horses have a lot to teach us about how to overcome devastating memories and replace bad experiences with good ones.

What comes more natural for a horse must be intentional for us. If we refuse to dwell on the hurts of the past and trust God to grace us with new experiences, we will move further away from the pain and into the possibilities of a great future.

Our memory and what we tell ourselves about what happened is where most of us get stuck. Not just because we have a story, but because our story is what we have chosen to believe.

Phoenix had an inexcusable experience, but for him, it was just an experience. As a result, he was able to live in the now. He didn't have a story to put the experience in perspective, so what happened yesterday was just an experience.

It is usually our story that causes the greatest problem. Too often we reach conclusions that are not always valid. Our story can tell us we are a failure, we are worthless, or we deserved what happened. Our story can change our identity.

Try to remind yourself that today's experiences may change everything. Try to loosen your grip on the story you have told yourself. Loosening your grip on the past allows you to reach out and grasp tomorrow.

Horses have some amazing lessons to teach us about moving beyond our past into a new life and incredible destiny.

Regardless of what has happened to us, we cannot step into the future if we are dragging the past behind us.

We all have a story that tells us things we wish were not true.

Even though our memories of the past may help us survive in one world, they will also be our greatest obstacle to living in a world that is vastly better. If you hold on to your history, you will always do it at the expense of your destiny. However, if you ignore your history, you will not recognize opportunities to change and overcome the past. Phoenix showed me that no matter how badly you have been treated, your past cannot be allowed to define you.

Horses don't seem to think about life as being fair or unfair. For some reason, they are able to move forward to the next thing and give tomorrow a chance. Horses have a unique ability to adapt, change, and put the past behind them.

Unfortunately, many of us are defined by a painful and unjust past. We build walls to protect ourselves from any further harm, but this only isolates us from a fulfilling life. If I had put Phoenix in a stall, he would have been protected, but in doing so, I would have empowered the abuse, allowing it to control him for the rest of his life. Instead, together we worked through the past to replace his pain with peace and purpose. The path from abuse to peace is not an easy journey, but a journey that is well worth the effort.

I will never forget Phoenix. He taught me that the abuse of the past did not have the power to define his future. I learned that, like a horse, I can look forward to amazing new experiences.

As I said earlier, we all have a story that tells us things we wish were not true. There is another story, however. A story worth telling yourself. It is the story of what God can do. It is the story of his plans for your life. The story of hope and healing will help move you forward.

The abuse of the past has no more power than the power you give it. You cannot get beyond the hurt of yesterday if you relive it today.

Today and tomorrow are filled with new opportunities for God to bless you with amazing open doors waiting for you step through them.

Chapter 5

Predators

Be well balanced [temperate, sober of mind], *be vigilant and cautious at all times; for that enemy of yours, the devil, roams around like a lion roaring* [in fierce hunger], *seeking someone to seize upon and devour.*

—1 Peter 5:8 (AMP)

Wild horses are constantly on the lookout for predators and are wired to be flight animals. Training horses can be described as the process of rewiring a horse's brain to process information in a way that allows them to move from fear to faith.

A good friend of mine and I were on an elk hunt in the mountains near Happy Jack, Arizona, as winter was beginning to settle in. We brought three horses—my friend's palomino roping horse, my five-year-old gelding, and my mustang Hershey. About two o'clock in the morning, we were awakened by commotion and noise from the horses in the corrals. Like any good, conscientious cowboys who want to get some sleep and stay warm, we shined a flashlight in the direction of the corrals and yelled, "Knock it off!" Things quieted down, and we went back to sleep. It wasn't until the morning that we realized a mountain lion had come into the corrals and attacked the horses.

The most visible horse in the moonlight was the palomino, and it seemed he was the target. He had claw marks on his chest and throat area, where the lion had made a good attempt to bring him down. Hershey, who had spent the first five years of her life in the wild, had claw marks on her back legs from kicking the lion. By the looks of things, the horses were able to join forces and win the battle. We followed the tracks of a wounded lion making its way back into the trees and apologized to the horses for not believing them.

From the moment they are born, wild mustangs learn that predators are an unfortunate part of their world. In the wild, predators hide in the brush, so wild horses must identify every sound. Predators try to move in from downwind or circle around, so the horse in the wild must identify every scent. Wolves and coyotes attempt to separate and devour, so horses learn that they are safer when together. Lions and bears wait for an opportune time to attack, so horses must be constantly on guard. Most predators slowly stalk their prey, so the horse learns to evaluate everything that moves or is out of place. If one horse within a herd spooks and begins to run, the others will follow. The conditions they live in often provide an environment where they are more vulnerable to predators. In drought, they must forage for food and water. In cold, they must band together and seek as much shelter as possible.

The horses that are born in the wild learn from a very early age that running is the best defense. They run when others run, they run from sounds, they run from scents, and they run from sights. Flight is the first line of defense, and the ones that run well survive.

I don't want my horse to become complacent or oblivious to the threat of predators, but on the other hand, I don't want my horse to be dominated by fear of predators when I am riding. There are some powerful parallels to this in the Christian life.

- Predators must be taken seriously.

  o *"That enemy of yours, the devil, roams around like a lion roaring [in fierce hunger], seeking someone to seize upon and devour"* (1 Peter 5:8, AMP).

- We must be alert and aware of our surroundings.

  o *"Be well balanced . . . vigilant and cautious at all times"* (1 Peter 5:8, AMP).

- The focus must be on God, not the predator.

  o *"Submit to God. Resist the devil and he will flee from you. Draw near to God and He will draw near to you"* (James 4:7–8, NKJV).

- We are much better together.

  o *"Not forsaking the assembling of ourselves together, as is the manner of some, but exhorting one another, and so much the more as you see the Day approaching"* (Hebrews 10:25, NKJV).
  o Horses desperately need to stay together. You don't find lame, sick, or young animals alone in the wild.

They cannot survive for long. A lesson that most of us need to be reminded of.

It would be foolish to want a horse that blindly dismisses predators and real dangers. Yet whenever we are in the saddle, we need to have confidence that our horse believes in us enough to go where we ask him to go.

The fact is, there are predators and dangers capable of destroying horses, and they instinctively know it. They must develop enough trust to believe that the person in the saddle is in control.

For us, we must remember that we are powerless to defeat the enemy without the presence of God directing our steps and working through our lives. *"Trust in the LORD with all your heart And do not lean on your own understanding. In all your ways acknowledge Him, And He will make your paths straight"* (Proverbs 3:5–6).

Courage to confront predators begins with a relationship. Something begins to transpire in those first few moments of training as the horse begins to associate a person with safety and rest. Nothing compares to the feeling I get when a horse begins to develop trust and refuses to leave my side. It never gets old. I think God would say the same thing about us. I don't think it ever gets old for God when someone who suffered through years of fear and defeat begins to seek him and wants more than anything else to simply be in his presence.

Every Christian has strong, determined predators that are intent on destroying him or her. The Bible does not tell us to dismiss or ignore the enemy. Instead, the Bible gives us clear instruction on what we are to do when the predators begin prowling around in our lives. James 4:7–8 (NLT) says, *"Humble yourselves before God. Resist the devil, and he will flee from you. ⁸ Come close to God, and God will come close to you."*

We were created to win battles. The barn is a safe place, but horses were not made for the barn. Horses were made to accomplish something outside the safety of the barn. They find their purpose in a world where there are predators.

The same is true for you and me. In church, we don't really see many challenges to our faith or worldview. But just as horses were not made for the barn, Christians were not made for the church. The church, like a barn, is where we find rest, nourishment, healing, and strength so we can fulfill our purpose beyond the walls and safety of the church.

Did you ever wonder why God tells us to be on the lookout for predators? I believe it is because he expects us to be out where predators are.

The safest horses are probably the least productive and most miserable. They have no battles to fight and no predators to look out for. Unfortunately, they have no victories.

Conversely, the safest Christians are probably the least productive and most miserable. No battles, no predators, and no victories.

One of my favorite quotes is from C. T. Studd. He said, "*Some want to live within the sound of church or chapel bell; I want to run a rescue shop, within a yard of hell.*" God calls us from the mundane, safe life to a life of battles and victories, a life of encountering and overcoming predators.

Chapter 6

Yes and Amen

For as many as are the promises of God, in Him they are yes; therefore, also through Him is our Amen to the glory of God through us.
                                        —2 Corinthians 1:20 (NKJV)

In horse training, we speak by what we do, not by what we say. What we do can be understood, and horses are masters at reading body language.

The old traditional way of training horses could be defined as saying no. We got the horse to pull back, so we could say, "That's wrong." We forced the horse to buck, so we could say, "Don't do that again." The horse had to listen to us (by our actions) screaming NO over and over again.

Horses are able to figure out when we are saying no, but there is a much more effective way of communicating.

Effective horse training is finding a positive way to speak the horses' language and get him to understand what we say. The horse has no way of knowing when he does something right, so we must learn to speak his language, or at least a couple of important words. I believe the most important word in regards to communicating with a horse is yes. *Yes* is the word I use more often than any other.

The Bible is filled with commandments and warnings regarding what we are to avoid, but the Bible is also filled with admonitions and guidance regarding what we *are* to do. We must retrain our spiritual ears to not just hear God say no but listen for him to emphatically say yes.

Learning how to say yes to a horse is by far the most single important tool I have.

In February of 2012, I was conducting gentling clinics in Apache Junction, Arizona, at the annual Lost Dutchman Days rodeo and wild horse adoption. Little did I know this particular event would have a lifelong effect on my future, and I owe it all to being able to say yes to a wild horse and getting her to understand what I had said. As the first clinic of the day began, the gate swung open, and a beautiful blue roan mare entered the round pen at a dead run. I was amazed at her beauty and boundless energy as she began running in circles around me. Soon she was understanding when I wanted her to change direction as she switched from clockwise to counterclockwise by recognizing simple cues. The very second she made the right choice, I did everything in my power to help her relax. After a few minutes she became noticeably calmer, her head began to drop, her eyes softened, and her gait slowed to a relaxing trot.

Thus began my language lesson. Every time her eyes met mine, I took all the pressure away. Soon we developed a basic language. No pressure meant peace, and peace meant yes. By the end of the clinic, she was glued to my side and even allowed me to gently slip a lasso around her neck and calmly lead her around the pen.

In the audience that day were a few key people from Arizona Correctional Industries who were looking for someone to develop and direct a wild horse inmate program at the Florence prison. A few months later I was offered the position, and I owe it all to a blue roan mare who simply figured out the word yes.

Any good horse trainer can get a horse to change. A great horse trainer gets the horse to want to change.

One of the challenges in horse training is finding a way to let the horse know when he does something correctly. Horses, like humans, look for peace. They don't like stress or discomfort and will look for ways to remove the pressure. For most horses, this means flight or fight. Horses can hurt themselves, hurt others, and destroy things in a frantic effort to escape danger or pressure, and they can also be lethal with their hooves and teeth if they have to fight. In order for a horse to understand yes, I do everything I can to give the horse room to figure things out by finding opportunities to say, "Good for you. You did that right."

Eventually a horse will actively search for the yes answer because he knows the answer is accompanied by peace. Once a horse realizes that *doing* the right thing will produce peace, or the release of pressure, he will begin *seeking* the right thing. A horse will do exactly what Psalms 34:14 instructs, "*Seek peace and pursue it.*"

In training horses, I find (and create) opportunities to say yes as often as I can, with my tone of voice or with gentle pats on the neck. I say yes by giving him as much peace as possible.

I believe every Christian will one day hear, "Well done, thou good and faithful servant." As Christians, we believe that one day God will clearly let us know that he is proud of our decision to follow him. However, I am convinced that if we listen, we will hear his still, small voice whisper, "Well done" throughout our lives. The challenge for us is to become more like the horse—seek peace and pursue it.

Countless untamed and untouched horses have followed trainers because they decided that peace was better than pressure and running in circles.

Sadly, multitudes of people have never experienced this kind of peace. For them, a normal life means living under constant stress and pressure. For multitudes of sincere men and women, peace is something they cannot even imagine. For many, peace is never pursued because it is never considered. If this sounds familiar, God is calling you to slow down, acknowledge him, and allow him to proclaim, "Yes and amen."

Chapter 7

A Solid Foundation

For no other foundation can anyone lay than that
which is laid, which is Jesus Christ.
                              —1 Corinthians 3:11

All good foundations involve the right process (they must be built). The foundation for building is much like the foundation for horses. It must be laid out and developed into a series of projects that support one another. If the foundation cracks or separates, the whole structure will collapse.

Too many horses are expected to perform at a level well beyond their foundation only to become frustrated and ineffective. Likewise, too many people are wanting to live better and accomplish things with their lives while neglecting the foundation. Unfortunately, many of us try to build a life of significance on a foundation with flawed character, only to become frustrated and ineffective.

A good foundation requires the right method. For building, the ground is leveled, footers are dug, and plumbing is roughed in to match the master plan. Often, I will watch the men in the wild horse inmate program as they work with a horse and then ask them to tell me what they are teaching the horse to do. It is always frustrating when I get a confused look or an "I don't know" answer. If you were to go up to a builder and ask the same question, you would probably be shown blueprints or at least get an explanation of how that specific procedure fits in to the finished product. The same principle should apply to horse training, and the same principle should definitely apply to life.

We need to ask ourselves the right questions, "What do I want the finished product to look like?" and "What am I doing to get the right foundation?"

Foundations require the right materials. Some foundations are made of concrete, where others are made of wood. The material affects how everything will be built. The same is true with horse training. The foundation has a direct correlation to function, stability, and purpose.

Briefly here is what I look for in building the right foundation for horses. The parallel to life is identical.

I want to build a foundation that gives me a way to communicate with the entire horse. It begins in the round pen as the horse learns to lower his head and bring his nose toward me. Eventually, every time I walk into the pen, he has learned to face me and gently come to me. It sounds simple, but I will build on that basic foundation for the rest of the horse's life. The foundation for getting the horse to calmly face me when I come into the pen is like getting the footers set and plumbing roughed in. If I build correctly, I end up with a horse that faces me when I come into the pen, puts its nose in my hands for haltering, and in a short period of time, will stop, go forward, turn right, and turn left before I ever get in the saddle. With that foundation, the possibilities are endless.

Imagine if you simply said, "God, today I want to learn to calmly face you and give you my undivided attention when you walk into the arena of my life." If that one thing became part of your foundation, you would find that slowly your direction, turns, and stops would begin to develop consistency and purpose as God opens doors of opportunity, allowing you to become more than you dreamed and accomplish what you were created to do.

Jesus emphasized the importance of a good foundation in Matthew 7:24–27 by comparing two houses, one built by a fool and one built by a wise man. The foolish man built his house on loose, sandy soil. The house stood for a while, well, at least until the storm came. The foolish man was focused only on the end result and wanted to avoid the process. The assumption often is that the foolish man built his house without a foundation. The truth is the foolish man built his house on a foundation that was weak. Sand is a foundation, but it is not a good one. Every person has a foundation. Some foundations are insufficient to serve a purpose, sustain weight, or handle storms.

Horses with foundations of sand are generally confused, and confusion makes them undependable. People with foundations of sand are exactly the same.

When I train horsemen and horsewomen, I emphasize the importance of building a good foundation. Just because a horse can be saddled does not mean it is ready for a saddle. Likewise, just because a horse can be ridden does not mean it is ready for a rider. There are things that should be done to prepare the horse so he can reach his full potential. The biggest struggle inmates face while training horses is building a solid foundation. Unfortunately, temptation to take shortcuts is not isolated to prison inmates but is common to horse owners everywhere.

Most horse trainers make their living fixing problems. The contradictory statements from owners are endless. "My horse is a great horse, but for some reason he won't stand tied"; "She is a good horse, but she runs off with me when I get on and won't stop"; "After I get the buck out of him, he is really a great trail horse"—the list could go on, but I am sure you get the point. When I am working with fixing a problem horse, I begin by trying to find the source of the problem. The majority of the time, the problem can be traced to the foundation.

Jesus tells us that the wise man built his house on the rock. When the storm came and the winds blew, the house stood firm.

Foundations must not only be built, but they must be built correctly. Digging down to bedrock requires hard work and a plan. But the result is something that will withstand the storms.

A horse with a solid foundation will perform well and be consistent under pressure. When I start a colt, I will not get in the saddle unless I am sure the horse is relaxed and knows how to yield to pressure. I make certain the foundation is solid as he moves forward, backward, and sideways with very light pressure.

Horses with foundations of bedrock are amazing. We generally recognize it under pressure when they go beyond our expectations, sometimes in the midst of a storm.

I watched a horse in competition making a turn to the right at a full gallop. Suddenly the saddle slipped to the side, and the rider went flying off as the saddle continued to spin around until it was hanging from the horse's belly. The horse immediately stopped, walked back to the cowboy, stopped, and stood as the saddle was readjusted. Now that's what I mean by a solid foundation.

Life would be significantly different if, when faced with a setback or challenge, we paused long enough to evaluate and inspect our foundation before we moved on. Many of our challenges and setbacks can be traced back to the foundation.

Taking shortcuts in life will almost always cost us down the road. We live in a world that tells us we should have whatever we want without a foundation or process. Taking shortcuts to reach the goal is no better for us than it is for horses. For instance, if a person wants people they love to see them differently and treat them with respect, they have two basic options. One is to work on always doing the desired thing when the people they care about are watching. Living an artificial life will work for a while, but like a poor foundation, it will eventually begin to crack and separate. The best option is to work on developing character and building a strong foundation to become the best person they can be. When we focus on the right thing, we develop strength that will stand through time and pressure.

There are exercises horse trainers use to keep the foundation strong. Even though the foundation has been built, we know that we must keep the foundation strong and guard against developing bad habits. Psalm 11:3 says, *"If the foundation is destroyed, what can the righteous do?"*

What areas in your life continue to fall apart or need repair? Chances are, the foundation needs work.

The good news is, you don't have to fix the foundation alone. I never expect the horse to fix his own foundation. I only ask that he yield to me and submit to a process of discovery and restoration.

If I will do that for a horse, how much more will God do that for you and me?

Chapter 8

The Power of One Thing

He tells us everything over and over, one line at a time, one line at a time, a little here, and a little there.

—Isaiah 28:10 (NLT)

Randy Carlson, author of *The Power of One Thing* (a book I highly recommend), would be a great horse trainer. Doing one thing, doing one thing well, and doing one thing consistently well is how I approach training horses.

One of the biggest problems in horse training and horsemanship in general is the overwhelming desire to arrive at the finished product without any process. Whether that is the desire to ride the horse or the desire to accomplish a maneuver, we must have a lesson plan on how to get there. One thing will get you there; everything will keep you stuck. If getting in the saddle and riding the horse is the priority, it will become the one thing, and we will miss the foundation that makes riding safe and enjoyable.

It is amazing how often one thing will change the whole horse. For instance, something as simple as getting the horse to carry his head lower can change everything about how the horse moves out and even how the horse stops.

Good horse training begins by getting one part of the horse to do one thing correctly. Every horse I start in training, whether a wild mustang or a gentle quarter horse, begins with the one thing. I never focus on the whole horse but on getting one spot to do one thing. Put enough spots together, and the whole horse is trained. Randy Carlson said, "*Every big accomplishment is preceded by lots of little, seemingly insignificant actions—resulting in the one big thing everyone sees.*"

I have done hundreds of clinics on gentling wild horses. The transformation is often amazing, and as a result, too many people think I did something mystical (hence the term horse whisperer). Generally, after forty-five minutes to an hour, the horse that was frantically running in circles is now standing calmly by my side or following me around. The end result is impressive, but most people miss the process that made it come together. The process is like a lesson plan and focuses on doing one thing at a time.

Here is a very short summary of the process of gentling a wild horse.

Since every horse knows how to trot, that's where I start. The horse moves around me clockwise, and then I simply change my position so the horse has to change directions to counterclockwise. Soon the horse has learned to yield to pressure and change directions while I try to not get run over or frustrate the horse (the first priority is trying to not get run over). Since every horse knows how to trot, I begin by asking him to do something I know he can do. Now I have something to build on.

The one thing is simply trotting forward, and without realizing it, the horse has allowed me to choose his direction and speed (even though speed is not the focus it is one of the results).

The next one thing is facing me as he learns to turn inside (toward me) when he changes directions. Every time he turns toward me, I remove as much pressure as I can, relax, and give him a little room. Soon he figures out that turning toward me is easier than turning away. Every time he turns toward me on cue, the pressure I put on him goes away, and his anxiety goes down. The one thing is now simply turning toward me while yielding direction. Every horse knows how to turn toward someone.

The next one thing is getting the horse to stop and face me. When he begins to change directions, I take a full step backward, giving him more room, and eventually he realizes he doesn't have to turn at all, so he stops halfway into his turn, which just happens to be facing me. I let him stand still and relax.

Before long, a horse that was frightened and running in circles has experienced a transformation into a horse that moves in the direction I want, turns toward me, stops, relaxes, and stands still. This is the foundation for everything that will follow.

If I expected a horse to calmly walk into the round pen for his first time, stop, turn toward me, and relax, I would be disappointed, and he would probably never learn to yield to my cues. But by doing one thing, doing it well, and doing it consistently well, the whole horse is changed.

With consistency, one thing will move from experience to learned behavior and eventually become a habit.

I have three expectations for every training session:

- No one gets hurt (the trainer or the horse).

- The horse is more relaxed at the end than at the beginning.
- At least one thing is learned or better.

Imagine if we treated each day or week this way. Wouldn't it be amazing if at the end of each week we could say, "This week no one got hurt, I have more peace, and one thing in my life is better." Put enough of those days or weeks together, and we have amazing growth and change.

Too often, we set big general goals such as, "I want to be a better person," "I want to be healthier," or "My goal is to be more like Christ." We can falsely assume we are achieving our goal because it is too general to accurately measure. Working on one thing or one spot can is measurable.

Aren't you glad, at the beginning of your spiritual journey, God didn't begin by giving you a list of things you needed to change? I have found that the Holy Spirit seems to work on one thing at a time and gives us peace when we get it right.

Chapter 9

Faith

Danielle Crooks
*Now faith is the assurance of things hoped for, the
conviction of things not seen.*
—Hebrews 11:1

Faith is the belief in something even if our natural senses can't confirm it is there.

Horses exhibit extraordinary faith. Every time I teach a horse to move across a tarp or go over a teeter-totter, I am amazed at their trust and faith. There is no way I can explain to an animal that the tarp is solid underneath or the teeter-totter bridge will stop on solid ground. The horse not only trusts me but he trusts me with his life. He has no way of knowing the outcome, but he takes a step forward.

Ultimately, I want my horse to have faith. I want the horse to know what I am going to do when I think about doing it. In horse training, we call this a precue, and it can be as simple as shifting our weight in the saddle. This may sound ridiculous, but it really works that way. If I am consistent with how I ride, the horse will pick up on small signals as I am planning to make a change. Responding to a shift in the weight in the saddle, for a horse, is much like you and I responding to God's still, small voice.

Faith is something that takes time and constantly grows. Eventually, I expect my horse to cross a river, but I begin with a shallow puddle or a small stream.

Jesus understood that our faith needs to grow. The vast majority of time, we have the ability to trust God with small things before we are faced with a situation that looks impossible. Imagine if Jesus invited Peter to step out of the boat and walk on water after the first week or even month. Peter had a front-row seat to the miraculous. He saw Jesus turn water into wine, feed multitudes of people, heal the sick, and the impossible become reality, until one day he was able to step out of a boat with nothing below him except deep water.

I want things that were once beyond the horses' wildest dreams to make sense.

We ask our horses to accept an entirely different way of living and thinking. We ask the horse to move from one kingdom controlled by fight or flight to a life dominated by gentleness and compliance. The road to success for a horse demands an enormous amount of faith.

The term *horse whisperer* has been used to describe trainers that employ a gentler approach in working with horses. Horse whispering is generally how the media describes what I do. I tend to avoid using the phrase *horse whisperer* because it can be interpreted that there is something mystical or magical about what I am doing.

When I train horses, my movements are generally slow, fluid, and deliberate. I speak softer (whisper) to keep myself calm, which translates to creating an environment that helps the horse learn. Horse whispering is a process of calmly, consistently repeating exercises using gentle, least-resistant techniques to gain a horse's trust and reward him with peace. When done correctly, this process will provide an atmosphere that allows the horse to develop what we would call faith.

We must be faithful and consistent for the horse to have faith. When the trainer is accepted as safe and believable, the horse is able to develop faith. For instance, to ask a horse to stop, I lean back in the saddle and put pressure on the bit by pulling back on the reins. When the horse responds by stopping, I release the pressure and sit back in the center of the saddle. If I suddenly changed my cue by leaning forward in the saddle, I would confuse the horse and lose credibility. However, if I remain consistent about leaning back and putting pressure on the bit, the horse will eventually understand that I'm asking him to stop the moment I shift my weight in the saddle.

It's important to release the pressure for the smallest change and slightest try. If I am wanting the horse to turn right, I will release pressure when the left foot takes a half step to the right and build on that. The horse develops faith that I will not change. I must be faithful before the horse can develop faith. Eventually I can touch the rein to the left side of the horse's neck, and he immediately moves right. We touch the horse with our foot on the right side, and he side passes smoothly left. The horse responds to slightest pressure because he has learned that we are consistent and believable.

That is very similar to how our faith in God is developed. God is not yanking us around beating us into submission. He is applying pressure in an area of life waiting for us to respond with the smallest change and slightest try. We are not expected to change everything all at once or be perfect. Faith is learning to hear the whisper of God and responding, as best we can, to yield to him.

Malachi 3:6 says, "*I am the LORD, and I do not change.*" God is consistent and believable. His faithfulness allows us to develop faith. Hebrews 10:23 (NLT) says, "*Let us hold tightly without wavering to the hope we affirm, for God can be trusted to keep His promise.*" Because we know God is faithful, we can begin to sense the still, small voice or the whisper of the Holy Spirit and respond with confidence.

We respond to the whisper of God because we know that he is consistent and believable. God's faithfulness is the foundation for our faith. If God says he will do something, he will do it, and if God thinks about doing something, he will do it.

My desire is to develop faith like a well-trained horse and learn to sense the precues when there is a distinct whisper or a shift in his weight in my life.

Hebrews 10:23 says, "*Let us hold fast the confession of our hope without wavering, for He who promised is faithful.*"

Chapter 10

Forgiveness

To forgive is to set a prisoner free and discover that the prisoner was you.

—Lewis B. Smedes

One of my favorite movies is *Warhorse*. The movie follows the life of a horse named Joey who is owned and loved by a young man on a poor farm in England. Joey eventually is placed in service fighting the Germans in the early 1900s. He experiences the horrors of war, is captured, and placed into service with the German infantry.

For me, the most moving scene was when Joey ended up tangled in razor wire and was slowly freed by two soldiers fighting on opposing sides of the battle.

In spite of all the trauma and abuse, Joey was able to move beyond the pain and cruelty. The movie is not only filled with emotion but it is believable. It is believable because horses can overcome incredible obstacles and, somehow, in a relatively short period of time, put it behind them and move forward.

I was raised on a working farm and ranch around seasoned cowboys who were great horsemen. They had a very aggressive method of training horses, and that method was the only way I knew to break a horse. The old cowboy style relied heavily, if not solely, on the fact that horses will forgive. For the most part, these cowboys were kind people who loved horses, and breaking horses by forcing them to submit was just a necessary means to an end. Ranchers often had limited time to break a horse, so it was done as quickly as possible. The horse, however, had to undergo drastic change and forgive. Cowboys and horse trainers never really thought of it that way, but if horses did not have a capacity to forgive, we would have had very limited success.

We all have things that have happened that we must overcome to become successful and productive. Few of us can compare to what a horse (in the old method of breaking) had to overcome.

Think for a moment of all the horse was forced to endure and eventually forgive for him to be productive. The standard method of breaking a horse began with no way of communication to help the horse understand what was expected. The horse was then subjected to a series of traumatic experiences. First the horse was tied up to a large post which caused panic. As he fought the confinement, he realized through pain that it didn't do any good, so eventually he gave up. Next, a horse blanket was thrown all over and around him until again he gave up. At that point, he was often introduced to the bridle by twisting his ear until he submitted to the bit and headstall. The blanket was then placed on his back, followed by a saddle, which was tightly cinched around his chest. When he stopped fighting, the saddle someone climbed on his back. Now he was tied tightly to a post with a combined weight of over two hundred pounds strapped to his back. Finally, he was released, and no matter what he tried to do the weight and discomfort stayed strapped to his back as he fought a piece of metal pulling against his mouth. And all this often occurred within the span of an hour.

Did I mention that horses are amazing? For a horse to overcome this level of trauma and become dependable is astounding. Their capacity to forgive is critical to their success.

The training methods I use and teach are vastly different from the methods I learned on the ranch. I do everything in my power to provide an environment where there is a basic communication established and gradually progress from there. However, regardless of how gentle I try to make the process, I still depend on the horse's ability to move beyond discomfort and distress in order to move forward.

Forgiveness is best described as releasing and letting things go. Most horses are masters at this, and few people understand it.

The root of *forgive* is the Latin word *perdonare*, meaning "to give completely, without reservation" (*perdonare* is also the source of our English *pardon*).

In horse training and horsemanship, the word *giving* is part of our terminology to describe a horse yielding to specific pressures. For horses, giving is the key to everything. It is no wonder that giving is at the very core of forgiving. If the horse does not give (or yield), he will not succeed. Likewise, if you and I don't learn to give, we will never reach our potential or succeed in life.

The very nature of the word *forgive* involves yielding for the benefit of personal peace and the benefit of others. When pressure is applied to the horse, he learns to move away from the pressure, or give to the pressure. The result is stopping, turning, moving forward, and any number of responses. Giving to pressure becomes the normal for the horse, and releasing pressure becomes our primary way of communication. Another way of saying giving to pressure would simply be letting go. As a trainer, I release pressure so the horse learns to release resistance.

I have spent years training inmates in the Arizona State Prison how to gentle and train wild horses. Most of these men have experienced devastating setbacks as a result of their actions and the actions of others. When I begin talking about moving forward, I don't refer to releasing as forgiveness because too often forgiving someone has the connotation of letting the person who hurt them get away with it. I do, however, use the example of removing themselves from the pressure that is pulling them back, and eventually I can help them define what forgiveness really is. The men who make it on the outside and become successful and productive are the men who discover how to release and put the past behind them. It is much easier for a horse than it is for a person.

Why can horses forgive easier than people? It is really quite simple and profound. As I said in chapter 4, horses have experiences, but they don't tell themselves a story to fit the experience.

People who have been hurt by others create a story, so the experience is placed into the desired context. We take our version of the experience, how we felt, what we thought, what others may have said, and we come up with a story. Sometimes our story is accurate but more times than not it is flawed.

Our story is what pulls us backward and keeps us in bondage.

I have talked with many men and women who have lived their lives trapped in the story they have told themselves. The story eventually defines them and certainly defines what happened to them. This does not in any way trivialize horrible or unfair things that happen in our past. We do need to, as best we can, separate the story from the experience.

I began with a reference to the movie *Warhorse*. There are a number of stories this horse could have told himself if horses did that. He could have determined that all people are cruel because the fact is some people were. He could have determined that he was worthless because he was treated as something to be used and abused. He could have easily told himself the story that life is not fair because a huge part of his would fit that narrative. Instead of stories, he had experiences.

He could overcome the horrible experiences by replacing them with new experiences. When people where kind to him and treated him with value, he had new experiences that gave him an opportunity for an amazing productive life.

Forgiveness is not an occasional act, it is a constant attitude. (Martin Luther King Jr.)

Chapter 11

Training the Horse You Have

Now is "the acceptable time," behold, now is "the
day of salvation."
—2 Corinthians 6:2 (NLT)

It would be much easier if training horses was more like building a home. Even though there are similarities, training horses is quite different from building anything.

When you build a house, you start with a good foundation and put up the walls. If you built it correctly and nothing catastrophic happened, you would not need to come back the next day and put the wall back up or fix something that has changed overnight. You simply continue building.

Unfortunately, many horse owners think of horse training like building a house. Horses, however, will always have a learning curve and will often revert to old behavior, comfortable patterns or simply gravitate to what they want to do.

Whether it is inmates learning to train horses in prison, people coming to clinics or me with my own horses, our struggles are the same. We too often assume once a horse does something correctly we can not only move on but we don't have to come back and fix anything.

Let me give you a common example. You have a horse that stands still for saddling and mounting, and one day you go out to ride and your horse has decided that today he will move when you are getting on. You say, "Knock it off . . . You know better than that," get on while he is moving around a little, and ride off. Before long your horse moves every time, and you just get more frustrated and tell your friends, "I don't know why he is acting this way. He knows better." For whatever reason, your horse has changed the program to fit what he wanted.

Training the horse you have today is simply making a decision that the horse's behavior, the very moment it occurs, is the only behavior you are aware of. When you go into the stall to catch your horse and his head goes in the corner while his butt is toward you, at that moment you are training a horse that needs to learn to face you each time you come into the pen.

Too often we try to train the horse we had yesterday, the horse a clinician had, or the horse your buddy has.

The only horse you can train is the horse that is present, and the only behavior you can address is the behavior that is being demonstrated at that very moment.

The horse may look identical to the horse you had yesterday, be in the same stall and have the same name, but for some reason today he is acting like a different horse. That's the horse you must train.

Training the horse you have today is not only being aware of the behaviors and what the horse has learned in the past but it is also being aware of what the horse does not yet know. You may see a maneuver demonstrated or accomplished by another horse owner or a trainer, and for some reason your horse will just not do that. Remind yourself that your horse is the horse that for some reason will not do what others have done, and rather than get frustrated by what your horse will not do, decide to train the horse you have.

It sounds simple, but it is profound in horse training and in life.

The horse I have must be evaluated by the behavior at that moment. If I focus on what the horse did right yesterday or what I want the horse to do tomorrow, I will not train the horse I have today. I must take into account what the horse learned yesterday because I know what the horse has accomplished, and likewise, I must have a set of goals for the future, but yesterday and tomorrow will not train the horse I have today.

The same principle can be applied to life. It is important to work on the person you are today. Our lives must be evaluated by this moment. The success of yesterday doesn't mean we won't face new challenges today.

Work on the person you are today. The life you have today must be evaluated by this moment. Just because you overcame something yesterday does not remove the battle today. Just because you drove to work yesterday with a great attitude does not mean today someone won't cut you off as they are texting, simultaneously eating a donut, and moving into your lane. Yesterday may have been a great day of maintaining a good attitude, but the horse you are training today needs to work on defensive driving, self-control and patience.

Work on the marriage you have today. If your marriage was great last year, last week, or yesterday, it doesn't mean you won't have to work on things today.

Marriage must be evaluated by the relationship you have today, the person you are married to today, and the person you are today. You cannot evaluate your marriage by what you had yesterday, what you expect tomorrow, and certainly not by what someone else appears to have.

Like horse training, work with the marriage you have today. Incidentally, men, it is never a good idea to refer to your wife as the horse you are training today. If so, the training will move into an entirely new dimension.

Work at the job you have today. Work can change from one day to the next. Some supervisors and coworkers may be unfair, responsibilities may change, and others may get promoted before you.

Determine to be the best employee you can be today.

Parent the children you have today. Parenting is one of the greatest challenges in life because the dynamics are always changing. One thing is for certain, the child you had yesterday will change tomorrow (figuratively and maybe literally) and often become someone you don't recognize. Be the best parent you can be today and work on what you can to improve.

Remember to train the horse you have and not the horse you had or the horse you wish you had.

Live the life you have and improve on it every day. You cannot live the life you used to have or the life you think you deserve.

> *Every day is a new day, and you'll never be able to find happiness if you don't move on.* (Carrie Underwood)

Chapter 12

Pressure

Here on earth you will have many trials . . . But take heart, because I have overcome the world.
—John 16:33

Yielding to pressure is the basis for all horse training. Pressure can come from the bit, reins, legs, vocal cues, and any number of other elements. We think in terms of the horse yielding to pressure, but it is much more complicated than that. Yielding to pressure is only half the equation. Each time we ask the horse to yield to something, we also expect the horse to resist something. If I cue the horse to move over a scary object for instance, the horse must choose to yield to my pressure while at the same time resisting the pressure to flee from the scary object.

There is a great parallel to horses and people when it comes to yielding and resisting.

The first thing I want to establish in training a horse is a habit of yielding to specific cues. Much of groundwork is to teach the horse through repetition that a specific cue from me requires a specific response from the horse.

Since Starbuck came out of the wild, he has willingly learned how to accomplish amazing tasks and overcome unbelievable pressure. I am constantly impressed by what he has learned and what he continues to learn. I can take this once wild horse on stage in auditoriums filled with people, lights, and sounds as he calmly waits for me to tell him what I want him to do. With a simple cue, he will willingly go over teeter totter bridges, stand on pedestals, and push against boards until they snap in two. If he were to be able to talk, his description of the training may be a little different than mine. He had to figure out what I wanted him to do as he processed how to deal with pressure. I am, however, glad he doesn't speak, because I am sure there are times I probably wouldn't like what he had to say.

God does this with his children all the time. Unfortunately, too often we miss God's groundwork in our lives because we think it doesn't make sense or we don't want to exert the effort.

Soldiers are a great example of yielding and resisting pressures. Men and women in the military are not placed in the heat of battle without boot camp and specific training. Much of basic training (boot camp) is tedious repetition. Drills have repetitious marching, cadence songs that drive you crazy, and routines that are continuously followed until you can perform them without thinking. And that is the point of routines. Pressure is what makes some soldiers, and pressure is what breaks others.

When I was in the military, we had to learn how to disassemble and reassemble an M-16 in the dark. Learning it was tedious, frustrating, and monotonous, but we knew the battlefield was not the place to start learning.

The pressure of the battle is not where we start learning how to yield to the pressure of those in command.

God knows this about us. That is why Paul wrote in 2 Timothy 2:3-5 (NLT), *"Endure suffering along with me, as a good soldier of Christ Jesus.⁴ Soldiers don't get tied up in the affairs of civilian life, for then they cannot please the officer who enlisted them."*

So it is with horses and people.

Horse training is filled with routines that are repeated until the horse doesn't even have to think about it.

Slight pressure from the legs can move a thousand-pound horse forward, backward, or sideways. Slight pressure from the reins can stop and turn a horse.

Once a small amount of pressure moves a horse, I can trust that he will be able to progress and resist the pressures that he will face. Yielding to one pressure is not an end in itself. Yielding to pressure from me is so the horse will be able to resist the pressures from other forces.

This principle has clear implications to the Christian life. We don't go through life yielding to every pressure that comes up. We learn that we need to yield to God, knowing that He will give us power to resist the opposing pressures. I believe spiritual maturity is defined just as much by the pressure we resist as the pressure we yield to.

When we yield to one pressure, we resist pressure in another area. Horses are powerful examples of this principle. We ask a horse to give to leg pressure to move forward. This is repeated thousands of times, and eventually the horse moves forward at the slightest movement. What began by pressure has now become as simple as a still, small voice, which we call a cue. That still, small voice becomes powerful enough to provide the strength and ability to resist unbelievable opposing pressures.

For instance, a clanking wooden bridge extending over a river would exert much more pressure than a slight tap with legs and slight movement of my hand, yet once trained, that's all it takes to move a horse across a bridge. When approaching a bridge, a horse has to resist the urge to lock up or flee and instead yield to my cue to move forward. Thankfully, I do not have to somehow match the opposing pressure of a bridge, canyon or raging river with equal force.

For us, yielding is where faith is walked out. When we learn to yield to God in the little things, we develop a pattern of obedience that gives us the courage to confront and overcome enormous obstacles.

Yielding develops principles and patterns that become more powerful than the opposing resistance. In short, yielding to the right pressure develops a horse's worldview. The horse learns what it should do, and what it should do becomes a powerful motivator.

John 16:33 says, *"Here on earth you will have many trials and sorrows. But take heart, because I have overcome the world."*

If I want my horse to overcome big obstacles, I will begin by putting small obstacles in his way. After a while, he learns to overcome the small obstacle, and eventually the big obstacle has no more power than the small obstacle had. My pressure can actually diminish because the pressure exerted by the obstacles fade in power until slight pressure from me actually is more than the pressure of a scary object. I think that's amazing! The horse learns that I will only ask him to do something I know he can succeed at. Pressure is simply my way of telling the horse, "We can do this."

I have always been impressed by cavalry horses that charged into battle with cannons, guns, and flags with a cue from their riders. God wants an army of men and women that will yield to the pressure of his Spirit and step out in faith knowing the *"He who promised is faithful"* (Hebrews 10:23).

When you feel the pressure of the still, small voice of God remember, it is his way of saying, "We can do this." Over time, the resistance from the outside has no control over the whisper of God.

Chapter 13

Renewing the Mind

And do not be conformed to this world, but be transformed by the renewing of your mind, so that you may prove what the will of God is, that which is good and acceptable and perfect.

—Romans 12:2

A little over a year after the wild horse inmate program began, the first news story was aired on the local NBC affiliate. A few inmates agreed to share their story.

This gave me a chance to hear them talk about the change in their lives and what they had learned about working with wild horses and burros. The reporter asked an inmate to describe what we do. He answered, "We are not breaking the horses . . . We are more like horse educators." I hadn't heard it put this way before, but I liked it. Horse educator is a great description for what a horse trainer should be doing. In horse training, we work on changing how a horse thinks. We spend time developing good habits that, through a process of repetition and consistency, become muscle memory.

When a horse comes into the program, he has developed a way of thinking about the world and specifically about people. He has fears and behaviors that are developed from genetics and environment.

Training a wild horse begins by changing how he thinks. The truth is, I don't teach the horse to do much of anything. He already knows how to do almost everything I want him to do. He knows how to stand still, walk, trot, and lope. The horse even knows how to accomplish advanced maneuvers such as flying lead changes and roll backs. What he doesn't know is what I want him to do and, even more importantly, why he should choose to do what I want.

The major focus in training horses is not how a horse acts but how a horse thinks. He comes in with a mind that thinks in a very particular way. My job as a trainer is to do everything I can to help the horse begin to think differently. Renewing the mind should be a journey rather than a destination.

For you and I, the challenge is to learn how to think more like God. The only way to think more like God is to read and apply what he says and what he thinks. Philippians 4:8–9 says, "*Fix your thoughts on what is true, and honorable, and right, and pure, and lovely, and admirable. Think about things that are excellent and worthy of praise.⁹ Keep putting into practice all you learned and received from me—everything you heard from me and saw me doing. Then the God of peace will be with you.*"

A horse that begins this process embarks on and incredible adventure into a new life, a journey that never ends.

I spent years conducting gentling clinics for the Bureau of Land Management at adoption events throughout the state of Arizona. Typically, I would work with twelve to fifteen wild horses over the course of a three-day adoption event. The horses would be brought in at random, and it was amazing to see the different temperaments and personalities.

The historic western town of Wickenburg, Arizona, was always one of my favorite adoption events, and because of a beautiful blue roan mare, it became one of the most memorable.

A big mare was driven up the alleyway and into a small round pen as I moved to the center, allowing her to begin trotting in circles around me. Every muscle in her body was tense. There was no question she was confused and afraid. She gave me her undivided attention, and soon she was turning toward me when I asked her to change directions. Fear diminished as she studied me intently. She figured out when I wanted her to turn and when I wanted her to stop. Then something happened that I didn't expect. About twenty minutes into the training, she stopped and looked at me. Her eyes softened as she dropped her head. She calmly walked to where I was standing and put her nose on my chest, allowing me to pet her while she stood quietly. Within fifteen minutes, she was haltered with a saddle blanket on her back.

The crowd thought I was amazing, and I overheard a lady say, "He is a *real* horse whisperer." I confessed to those attending that this was not normal behavior and I certainly was not that good.

Something changed in the mare's thinking, and consequently she made a decision to trust me. Every time she turned toward me or faced me and stopped, all the pressure went away. She made the connection between what I was trying to do and what she was doing. Soon she figured out that I was not the source of her running in circles but rather the source of her resting and having peace. She decided she wanted to stop running and be closer to the source of peace.

Renewing the mind is much like that for you and me. We can run in circles wondering why God is doing this to us, or we can begin responding to him and realize he is just waiting for us to understand, stop running, and rest in his peace.

Like the horse, we think a certain way because that's how we are wired. Our genetics and experiences give us the lens through which we see the world.

We are transformed by the renewing of our minds as we realize that God is not here to make us run in circles but to give us peace and a life worth living.

I like the translation of Romans 12:2 in the New Living Translation of the Bible. It says, *"Don't copy the behavior and customs of this world, but let God transform you into a new person by changing the way you think. Then you will learn to know God's will for you, which is good and pleasing and perfect."*

Horses take their cues from other horses. If one runs, they all run. Renewing the mind begins when we decide we are not going to take our cues from the behavior and customs of this world, and we recognize that God has the answers for life, purpose, and peace.

> *Life isn't about finding yourself. Life is about creating yourself.* (George Bernard Shaw)

Chapter 14

Purpose

"For I know the plans I have for you," says the LORD, *"to give* [not sure what needs to be changed here. seems to be a typo in the first draft, and I'm not sure what you want to say] *you a future and a hope.*

—Jeremiah 29:11

The two most important days in your life are the day you are born and the day you find out why.
—Mark Twain

I am convinced that few people ever take the time to simply ask, "Why am I here?" Millions of people live their entire lives not knowing why they were born and what will give them a passion and fulfillment.

This idea of purpose forces us out of the mundane and propels us higher as we attempt things that seemed beyond our reach. It frees us from the chains of emptiness and discontent. It was Henry David Thoreau who said, "The mass of men lead lives of quiet desperation," and his words resonate more today than when he wrote them.

Horse trainers are often confronted with forced purposes that don't always fit the horse. I regularly hear a well-intentioned grandparent ask if I can train a high-spirited mustang for their grandchild because they watched a movie about a wild horse that bonded with a child. Or someone who wants me to turn a chronically lazy horse into a performance horse.

People too often make plans for their horses without taking the horse's conformation, intelligence, and temperament into account.

The two main enemies of finding a horse's purpose are plans that don't match the horse and plans that are not developed. Sometimes the plans just don't match the horse, and as a result, there are good barrel horses that would make excellent ranch horses, good dressage horses that would make amazing gymkhana horses, and underachieving roping horses that would be awesome trail horses, to list a few.

On the other hand, there are those horses that can do amazing things but never have the opportunity to develop their strengths. People are like that too.

Growing up on the ranch, we had about a dozen thoroughbred racehorses. Since I loved exercising the horses and going to the tracks, I decided I wanted to be a jockey. Since jockeys average a little over 5 feet tall and about 118 pounds, my dream of becoming a jockey came to a gradual halt, and by age 12, the dream was gone. Had I tried to hang on to that dream, now at 6 feet tall and 180 pounds, I would be very frustrated and unsuccessful.

Purpose is putting together your strengths, gifts, passion, and calling to become more than you thought possible. Purpose is more of a path than it is a destination. Had I not wanted to be a jockey, I may not have applied myself to riding high-energy horses. Purpose does not have to perfectly fit your natural strengths, gifts, and passions. However, it must fit your calling. Your *calling* is harder to define than your personality or your giftedness. Moses wasn't an eloquent speaker (not an obvious choice to lead God's people out of Egypt), yet he was called for that specific purpose. Peter seemed to be rather angry and impetuous (questionable qualities for the first leader of the church), yet he was called to build a church of power and stability. Paul was a proud Jew on a mission to stamp out the church (not an obvious choice to bring the gospel to the gentiles), yet he was not only called to bring the gospel to the gentiles, but he wrote the majority of the New Testament.

Pablo Picasso said, "*The meaning of life is to find your gift. The purpose of life is to give it away.*" Your calling is what God has for you to do, and it will enable you to exceed your natural abilities and overcome your weaknesses. Discovering your gift and learning how to use it to make this world a better place becomes more than just a purpose. It becomes a *calling*.

The best kids horse I have ever owned was a little mare named Hershey. I picked her up in 1994, only a few months after she had been captured out of the wild. When threatened, she would strike out with her front hooves or whirl around and try to kick. However, once she learned to relax and respond, there was nothing I asked her to do that she refused. When carrying a child, she was careful to take smaller steps and to stand perfectly still when they got on and off and seemed to sense when they were frightened as she calmly came to a stop. Had I tried to determine purpose within the first few weeks, I would have ruled out carrying small children around. But Hershey had a calling. I owned her for six years, and she went on to live the rest of her life teaching children how to ride horses.

A central part of what a horse trainer does is finding ways to help the horse achieve its purpose. A good horse trainer always has a plan. He or she thinks about what the horse is doing, the disposition, the build, and the pedigree. Sometimes the plan has begun before the horse is ever born, and sometimes the plan is developed as the horse moves forward in training.

Jeremiah 29:11 says, *"For I know the plans that I have for you,' declares the Lord, 'plans for welfare and not for calamity to give you a future and a hope."* I have always found this verse to be reassuring. God has the plan, so he will arrange the timing and the process if I will only yield to him. It makes my job a lot easier.

In horse training, a horse does not have to spend any time trying to figure out his purpose. He simply must yield to the pressure and submit to the process and discover what he can do. You and I are not the ones that ultimately determine our purpose. Like a horse, we must yield to the process and discover why we are here.

Finding your purpose is not much different than a horse arriving at his. Since God knows the plans he has for you, it makes sense to surrender to the process he has begun, and it makes no sense to insist on the process that you have chosen.

Like horse training, finding your purpose is not simply rushing forward to arrive at the end result but rather understanding that the path brings you to the desired destination. For instance, there are literally hundreds of small things that come together in the development of a good rope horse. Each one is critical to what the horse is to become. The horse is to learn grow and yield.

Finding your calling begins when you understand that purpose is a path not a destination.

Training horses often has a moment when the horse lets you know it can do things that you didn't expect or do things easier than you imagined. It is as if the horse is saying, "This is what I was born to do."

That's the way life often is. We don't determine our purpose—we discover it. Purpose is a path, sometimes rocky and sometimes winding, but ultimately leading us to our destiny.

Chapter 15

Developing Good Habits

*So we must not grow weary in doing good, for in
due time we will reap, if we do not give up.*
                                    —Galatians 6:9

It is ten times harder to break a horse of a bad habit than to teach a horse a new one. Wouldn't it be great if that principle were only true with horses? The majority of horse trainers make a significant portion of their income because people let horses develop bad habits.

Like people, all horses have behaviors and some behaviors become habits. A behavior is the manner in which a horse acts while a habit is something the horse has been taught or allowed to do repetitively until the behavior becomes automatic.

I own three horses, all of which have good and bad habits. My smallest horse, Dusty, has the habit of chasing my biggest horse, Stetson, away from his food. Stetson has the habit of avoiding conflict and walking away to another manger. It began as a behavior. At feeding time, Dusty would kick at Stetson, and there would be a few moments of conflict before Stetson would reluctantly walk away. Over time, there was no conflict or resistance at all. Now, Dusty waits until the other horses are fed to calmly walk over to where Stetson is eating, slightly pin back his ears back, and Stetson walks away.

It is not a terrible habit, but I always feel sorry for Stetson. What began as simply avoiding conflict has become an automatic behavior.

For years it has been widely reported that it takes thirty days to develop a habit. This number comes from a study in the 1950 by Dr. Maxwell Maltz. Dr. Maltz concluded that it took twenty-one days as a minimum, depending on the person and the behavior to develop a habit. Unfortunately, the minimum soon became the standard. Recent studies conclude that it takes an average of sixty-six days to form a new habit. The magic number of thrity days so often reported sets more people up to fail than succeed.

In horse training, it is foolish to set a specific number of days or hours to complete a certain lesson. Some horses may have mastered a routine in an hour while another may take days. Every horse is unique.

The same is true in life. Many people become discouraged because they have an ambiguous number that comes from a book or someone else's experience. Remember that you are uniquely you.

Good habits are not determined by a calendar, but by behavior, that has become automatic.

I don't know about everyone else, but for me, it seems that bad habits develop much quicker than the good ones, and changing them is much more difficult and takes longer. It may take only two days to develop a bad habit, but it feels like lifetime to change it to a good habit.

Good horse trainers understand that habits are the cornerstone to training horses. Horses that do things automatically are fun to watch and a pleasure to ride. I have seen John Lyons walk into a huge pasture where his horses were grazing, and when he calls them, they come running directly toward him in unison and in the right order from left to right.

I don't think John went to the pasture one day, called the horses, and as they ran toward him, he thought, "Wow, that's a neat surprise." John spent hours developing this response with each individual horse until they didn't have to think about it. It became their normal or habit.

Just like with horses, developing good habits takes time, consistency, and repetition. I am not going to wake up one day with a good habit and say, "Wow, that was a neat surprise."

Most of us have good habits and bad ones. I am an early riser. I don't have to set an alarm and couldn't sleep in if I wanted to. I developed a habit from living and working on the farm for years. I am glad I developed that habit and enjoy getting up early. However, I habitually drive nine miles per hour over the posted speed limit on the freeway. When I was a police officer, our policy was to write tickets when drivers exceeded ten miles per hour over the posted limit on freeways. Nine miles over the speed limit eventually became a habit for me, and even now I find that habit hard to break.

Some habits are dangerous and self-destructive, while others give us our strength and identity. We must continue to work on developing and reinforcing the good habits while we continue to avoid and break the bad ones.

How long it takes to develop a good habit isn't what is important. It doesn't really matter whether it takes thirty days or a year. The point is habits take work and consistency.

You don't need to know how long it will take. Every journey has to begin with day 1.

Where the quote below originated is the subject of some debate, but the truth of the quote is profound.

> *Watch your thoughts, they become words;*
> *watch your words, they become actions;*
> *watch your actions, they become habits;*
> *watch your habits, they become character;*
> *watch your character, for it becomes your destiny.*

Chapter 16

Your Incredible value

I will give thanks to You, for I am fearfully and wonderfully made; Wonderful are Your works, And my soul knows it very well.

—Psalm 139:14

A few years back, I spoke at Heart Cry Cowboy Church in Queen Creek, Arizona, about the value God places on our lives. I emphasized that my horse, Stetson, was a $125 mustang, but the saddle he was wearing cost me $500.

At that time, the best saddle I owned was a Circle Y roping saddle, and it was that saddle I used for the illustration. I never once thought that my horse didn't deserve to wear a saddle that cost four times as much as he did. Instead I put my best on him because he was worth more to me than the saddle.

One of the points in the message was that God does not treat us according to a value the world has placed on us or the value we have placed on ourselves; instead, he values us enough to put his very best on us and in us. The response to the message was very encouraging, and I spent quite a bit of time talking and praying with those who had seen themselves as worthless and undeserving of what God had for them.

That night, my wife and daughter loaded the horse in the trailer and set my saddle in the bed of my pickup before they went home. By the time I left, it was dark, and I was running late, so I jumped in the truck and took off. Soon it felt as though the trailer locked up. I pulled over and got out of the truck to discover that I hadn't put the tailgate up and the remaining pieces of my favorite saddle were wedged under the axle of the trailer. Even though I had bought it used, it was the best saddle I had ever owned.

On the way home, I decided I wouldn't let this event ruin my day. After all, the service had gone well, and it was just a saddle.

A couple of years later, I met the regional sales representative for Circle Y Saddles. He had attended a couple of the cowboy churches and clinics in Florence, Arizona. He asked if I would consider being one of Circle Y's local trainers of influence, and in return, I could pick out a brand-new saddle of my choice. Now every time I put the saddle on my horse, I am reminded of the message of our value and how God even provided a better saddle to replace what had been destroyed.

Something that had great value to me became worthless, yet God provided something far greater. He took a loss and turned it into a great gain. The parallels to life speak volumes. Now I saddle my $125 horse with a $2,000 saddle. Even though my horse cannot comprehend the value of what I place on him, I will continue to ensure it is my best. That is exactly what God does with you and me. God puts his best on you because his best is all he has. I will never comprehend the value of my soul or the value of what God has placed on me and in me.

One of my favorite passages in the Bible is Isaiah 61:1–4, "*The Spirit of the Lord GOD is upon Me . . . the LORD has anointed Me To preach good tidings to the poor; He has sent Me to heal the broken-hearted, To proclaim liberty to the captives . . . the opening of the prison to those who are bound; . . . To comfort all who mourn . . . To give them beauty for ashes, The oil of joy for mourning, The garment of praise for the spirit of heaviness; That they may be called trees of righteousness, The planting of the LORD, that He may be glorified.*"

I don't believe every horse owner must have new or expensive tack, deluxe stalls, and manicured pastures. I do, however, believe that every horse owner should strive to give their horse the best they have. Too often people purchase or adopt horses because they are cheap and then treat them cheaply.

When I see a horse with tack that is worn-out and uncomfortable, a saddle that doesn't fit, matted, ungroomed coat, and hooves that have grown out, I assume the horse will perform down to the expectation placed on him. If we treat a horse cheaply, we cannot expect the horse to develop quality.

I am not suggesting you cannot have horses with a limited budget. Growing up, we were very poor. All our saddles were old, and the stalls were in constant need of maintenance and repair. Yet we were careful to provide the best we possibly could.

God isn't poor and doesn't have cheap stuff to place on us and in us. His best is pretty amazing. He will not provide you with junk because he simply does not own junk. He puts his best on you and places his best in you because of the value he has placed on your life. God gives us his best in order to give us every opportunity to accomplish more we ever dreamed.

I have met people who have experienced setbacks, failure, and abuse. As a result, many have reached the conclusion that they are worthless and have a difficult time accepting the grace and blessings of God. Living your life as though you are worthless is an insult to God.

In our culture, it is sometimes difficult to live above the cheapness that is offered as an identity. Anthony Carmona said, *"Social media websites are no longer performing an envisaged function of creating a positive communication link among friends, family and professionals. It is a veritable battleground, where insults fly from the human quiver, damaging lives, destroying self-esteem and a person's sense of self-worth."*

In today's world, we are too often given what society has chosen for us, only to find it is not only junk but has placed on us a value that God never intended.

In 1 Peter 1:18, the Bible says that we were *"not redeemed with corruptible things like silver and gold but with the precious blood of Christ."* We may never understand the fullness of what that means, but God will continue to supply us with His best because He does not possess anything less.

God puts his best on us. He puts His best in us. He works His best through us.

You Are Adopted

Whose you are has an incredible effect on *who* you are, which profoundly affects your sense of value.

Two of my horses were adopted from the BLM. Even though they are completely unaware of it, I took responsibility for their care and safety. My commitment to these two horses does not even come close to the commitment God makes to you and me.

Romans 8:15 (NKJV) states, *"For you did not receive the spirit of bondage again to fear, but you received the Spirit of adoption by whom we cry out, 'Abba, Father.'"*

This verse always meant a lot to me. When I was seven years old, I (along with two brothers and two sisters), were removed from our home. Three years later, I was living with grandparents and was the only one that had not been adopted. For me, adoption meant that someone wanted you.

You Have Been Purchased

The purchase price of a horse is usually only a small portion of the cost. The time, care, feed, and transportation are all part of our commitment.

Remember that you have been purchased by God. It has cost him a lot, and he will follow through on his commitment.

God Has Placed His Best in You

The Bible says that Christ is in us, we have a new heart, and God has placed gifts and power in each of His children. That's pretty awesome.

In 1 Corinthians 3:16 (NKJV), it states, *"Do you not know that you are the temple of God and that the Spirit of God dwells in you?"*

God Has Placed His Best on You

"The Spirit of the Lord is upon me" (Isaiah 61:1).

There is perhaps nothing that indicates value as much as what you carry or pull.

A race horse in the Kentucky Derby, a team roping horse in the national finals, and a Clydesdale in a parade are all defined somewhat by the weight and what they do with it.

The same is true with people.

Sadly, there are also people who are weighted down with trash. They carry it around every day, and it eventually defines their value.

Choose to "put on the Lord Jesus Christ" (Romans 13:14) and carry him into every facet of your life. Not only will your value skyrocket, but you will find that you have exchanged brokenness for healing, bondage for freedom, ashes for beauty, sadness for joy, and heaviness for praise.

In the Old Testament, one of the main words for *glory* is translated "weight." The glory of God is the weight of God. We carry his presence. Talk about incredible value!

> *Finally, my brethren, be strong in the Lord and in the power of His might. Put on the whole armor of God.* (Ephesians 6:10–11)

Chapter 17

Stopping with Energy

Josh Lyons
Depart from evil and do good; Seek peace and pursue it.

—Psalms 34:14

As a horse trainer, one of the things that drives me crazy is a horse that comes to a stop slowly. I train my horses to stop by training them to back up. Rather than having the horse think about applying the brakes, I want them to think about shifting into reverse. Once they do this, they stop with energy. Imagine if a car was made without brakes and instead only had forward and reverse. That's the way I want my horses to think.

I believe that God wants us to stop with that kind of energy, and when we slowly come to a stop, I think it drives him crazy (figuratively, of course).

When I was a kid, we played a game called red light, green light. There was a starting line and a finish line. As soon as "green light" was yelled, everyone quickly walked forward. Then as soon as "red light" was yelled, everyone had to stop. If you even went forward half a step more, you had to return to the starting point. Eventually everyone would stop with energy.

Stopping with energy is what we should expect from horses, and for us, it is the key to living a successful life.

One of my favorite rodeo events at the national finals is calf roping. The ropers that compete are talented and impressive, but the horses that compete at this level are truly remarkable. These horses are not only athletic but they have unbelievable response to the slightest cue. They are amazing to watch from the box to the finish. But what really impresses me is their stop. Roping horses stop with energy. As soon as the rope leaves the roper's hand, the horse is already beginning to shift gears.

Reverse is really a stop with an exclamation point.

Reining horses performing a sliding stop are great examples of stopping with energy. Josh Lyons once told me that, when done correctly, a sliding stop should feel kind of like riding into melted butter. I will confirm that when I do it correctly. In the meantime, I will take his word for it.

Both the roping horse and reining horse are taught to read subtle cues from their rider. This is how God wants us to stop. Not just with energy, but sensing the still, small voice of the Holy Spirit and recognizing a shift in the weight.

Imagine if, with energy, we could:

- Stop before we say something we shouldn't say
- Stop when someone is hurting and we can offer help
- Stop thinking destructive thoughts
- Stop before we do something we shouldn't do
- Stop and redirect our focus to attending others' needs

Too often, I slow down but don't come to a full stop, or by the time I do stop, I have already gone too far. Consequently, I miss opportunities to help others or avoid costly mistakes.

A friend of mine told me about a horse he had when he was a kid. According to him, the horse would refuse to stop. No matter how hard he would pull on the reins, the horse simply would not stop. So in desperation, he would aim the horse at a tree or wall to get him stopped. Now, as a trainer, that sounded pretty ridiculous, until I thought of the spiritual application to my own life. I wondered how many walls and trees God had to steer me into to get me to stop.

I spent a week riding one of Josh Lyons's reining horses in Cross Plains, Tennessee. It helped me as a trainer to get the feel of a spin, flying lead change, and sliding stop. The horse made me look better than I was, and I learned some great lessons about stopping with energy.

When I got home, I started training my horse Starbuck to do a sliding stop. It wasn't long before he was getting the hang of it, and soon he seemed to enjoy it. Once in a collected lope, I could feel him anticipating a shift in my weight and a slight movement of my hand. As soon as my weight shifted, he would slide to a stop, drop his head, and start backing up. I wish I were that attentive to the still, small voice of God.

Stopping with energy does not happen by accident. It requires repetition and practice. Stopping with energy is the result of consistency. Consistency is doing the same thing the same way so the horse is clear on expectations. Stopping with energy has amazing rewards.

For the horse, and for us, stopping with energy keeps us out trouble and makes the journey through life safer and more enjoyable.

Chapter 18

When Things Fall Apart

From the end of the earth I call to You when my heart is faint; Lead me to the rock that is higher than I.

— Psalm 61:2

In 1998, my dad and I took four horses and packed in to a remote area in the Arizona Bloody Basin wilderness for a mule deer hunt. Our camp was at the end of a steep canyon where Houston Creek joined the Verde River. The abandoned steep road winding into the bottom of the canyon served as a decent trail. We packed in tents, rifles, bedrolls, and enough food to last a week. Being there with dad was a little surreal.

Dad had been coming to this remote spot since he was a boy and first brought my brother and me down into the canyon when I was seven. Some of my favorite memories were formed in this canyon on the banks of the Verde River. Even though I had been there more times than I could count, it never seemed to get old.

Now at forty-three years old, the familiar sound of the river gently lulled me to sleep.

Early Friday morning, we saddled up our horses and set out on a trail that wound up over a precipitous granite ridge that descended to the river crossing. I rode a part-draft BLM gelding named Outlaw while leading a packhorse. As Outlaw and I topped the ridge, I couldn't help but notice the sheer drop-off and sound of the rushing water below. I had walked over the trail many times, but on horseback, the view was even more amazing.

Suddenly, Outlaw lost his footing, and as his feet scrambled for traction, he reared up in an attempt to turn around. At that point, I knew we were going over.

I kicked myself free from the stirrups and dove from the saddle, hitting the granite with a thud as I started sliding headfirst down the side of cliff. I could hear Outlaw sliding and rolling toward me, and I remember clearly thinking, "This is how I will die."

I vaguely remember the moment Outlaw's 1,400-pound body caught up with mine. Everything went black as I was knocked unconscious the moment he rolled over me. When I came to, I could hear my dad yelling my name and trying to make it down to where I was lying. I struggled to get up and finally was able to stand. Once on my feet, I looked down to the bottom of the cliff. Outlaw was upside down in a pile of boulders with all four feet in the air. I was certain he was badly injured, and I mentally prepared myself for what seemed inevitable. I would have to put him down.

I slowly limped down to where he was laying. He looked at me with bewildered but big kind eyes as I inspected him. Surprisingly, I couldn't find any significant injuries. I petted him for a moment then gently tugged on the reins to see if he could free himself. I watched as he miraculously wriggled free from the rocks and stood up.

By this time, blood had soaked though both my gloves and my right pant leg. I knew I was hurt but had no idea how badly, and it would be two days before I would get medical help.

I somehow managed to get in the saddle, and this amazing horse, which had every reason to distrust my judgment, carried me for the next six hours through three river crossings, up canyons, and over mountains.

After a few hours of riding, I started going into shock as a result of internal injuries and crushed, severed muscles. Outlaw carried me on as I fought excruciating pain and uncontrollable chills and shaking. To this day, I wonder how much pain he was in because he never showed it. Late that night, we made it to an old-line cabin called Horse Camp.

As I lay there in the warmth of the cabin, the chills and shaking began to subside. With the crisis behind me, I was able to reflect on what had happened earlier in the day. It was only then I realized that there was no way I should be alive.

Having a close call with death tends to give us perspective.

Perspective reminds us that we should be grateful and often reminds us that there are definitely worse things. Surviving a horse rolling over you on a rugged, remote mountain is easier than surviving the death of someone you love, trying to pick up the pieces after a divorce, battling a life-threatening disease, or the helpless pain of a watching your child making choices that could destroy their lives and future.

The pain when things fall apart in life seems unbearable, and the recovery often seems impossible. Yet we have no option but to get up and do what we can to move forward. Whether it is limping or crawling, we have to press on.

When things fall apart, we don't have time to think about what or why or how. Instead we move into survival mode. Survival mode is not always a bad thing. However, if surviving is the way we live the rest of our lives, we stop living. Surviving the ordeal is the first step. The next step is when you realize that your world just went black and you hurt all over. At that point, you have no option but to get up with a determination to see what you need to do to move forward. We have to pick up the pieces and limp, walk, or ride away. Survival mode should only last as long as it takes us to realize we have survived. We cannot wait until the pain is gone or we feel good. The sooner we can move away from the cause, the sooner the pain will diminish.

The pain can be excruciating, but we can't afford to give ourselves any other option than moving forward. We may walk with a limp, but we must walk. For months following my accident, I had to spend hours each week in physical therapy. I dreaded the pain associated with getting better, but I knew without that pain, I would have to live with limitations and greater pain.

Shock is when our body starts shutting down so it can deal with the trauma. When shock begins to take hold because of internal injuries, we must do our best to go on. When we are in shock, we don't function well, and life is a little blurry. Whether physical pain or emotional pain, shock will subside with time, support, and healing.

The greatest internal injuries are those that are emotional, but they too will pass as we begin to heal and take one day and one step at a time. We may walk a little different, but we will walk.

I wish I were more like Outlaw. Without hesitation, he went over the same steep trail he had lost his footing on. He stood still as I worked my way back into the saddle, and to top it all off he carried me for hours. Horses have an amazing ability to recover when things fall apart. Horses seem to be able to live in the present, even if the past was earlier the same day.

If I see the road ahead as impossible, because in the past things fell apart, I will never move toward healing and wholeness.

Chapter 19

Good Enough

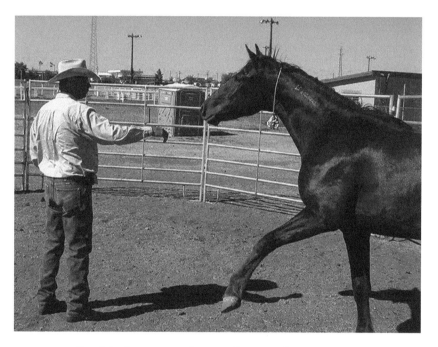

*Good is the enemy of great. Few people attain great
lives, in large part because it is just so easy to settle
for a good life.*

—James C. Collins

Great horse trainers rarely have good horses, because great horse trainers strive for great horses. In Mark 8:22–25, the Bible gives us an example of something that was good, but not good enough.

When they arrived at Bethsaida, some people brought a blind man to Jesus, and they begged him to touch the man and heal him. Jesus laid his hands on him and asked, "Can you see anything now?" The man looked around. "Yes," he said, "I see people, but I can't see them very clearly. They look like trees walking around." Then Jesus placed his hands on the man's eyes again, and his eyes were opened. His sight was completely restored, and he could see everything clearly.

Jesus asked this man if he could see anything. Wouldn't he know? I believe that Jesus asks questions because we need a chance to learn something.

I have no doubt Jesus knew the answer to his question before he asked.

I believe he asked the question because the disciples (and of course you and I) needed to know that God doesn't stop working on us just because we are better, and we should not be satisfied with anything less than what God has for us.

Good enough usually means that we have decided to stop working on something because it is difficult or too time consuming. When things are much better than they used to be, we become satisfied with average or even a little less than average. I don't want an average horse, and I certainly don't want to be content living a mediocre life.

Those who accept a mediocre existence become content with second-rate lives and don't even think about the possibility of excellence.

All of us can become content with something that is good enough and miss excellence. We live lives that can be okay, and soon okay becomes the standard. We can end up missing God's best because we are better than we used to be. Or we can find someone to compare ourselves to in an attempt to make us look better. In 2 Corinthians 10:12, it says, "When they measure themselves by one another, and compare themselves with one another, they do not show good sense" (NRSV).

Owners often limit horses that have great potential. Trainers are often satisfied with far less than what the horse is capable of. "Good enough" is one of the greatest enemies of horse training, and as a result, we are content with a horse that never achieves greatness. A wonderful horse that won't trailer-load or a great horse that refuses to stand for a saddle usually has an owner that either does not know how to help the horse be better or has settled for "good enough."

I don't want to have a better wild horse. I want a horse that has yielded to a process that has resulted in a completely different horse with a new life and new destiny. Good enough will never produce that.

Jesus didn't come to make me good enough. A better-lost person is not God's goal for my life or yours. He came that I might have an abundant life. That abundant life is only possible as I move from the world dominated by my old nature and move into his kingdom. Someone once said, "Your past may explain you, but it will never excuse you." This is true with horses and certainly with people.

The Bible says a lot about living lives of excellence. As with so many other things, lives of excellence begins with what you think. Philippians 4:8 says, "*One final thing. Fix your thoughts on what is true, and honorable, and right, and pure, and lovely, and admirable. Think about things that are excellent and worthy of praise.*" Romans 12:2 (NLT) says, "*Don't copy the behavior and customs of this world, but let God transform you into a new person by changing the way you think. Then you will learn to know God's will for you, which is good and pleasing and perfect.*"

If a horse is only expected to do what he can do, he will never become anything more than he is. Moving beyond good enough for horses is a constant progression toward perfection. Good horse trainers always think about what is possible, not what is easy.

If you only do what you can do, you will never be more than you are today.

The inmates I work with to train horses will often chuckle if someone says "Good enough" around me because they know what will follow. I will always ask why something is good enough and what will it take to make it great. The problem with "good enough" is it implies that one is accepting something less, something incomplete. If you heard someone's wife describe her husband as "good enough," you would immediately wonder what was wrong with the husband or the marriage. Why do we accept "good enough" in horse training, or worse, in life and personal growth? One of the greatest enemies to spiritual growth and development is "good enough." Never accept anything less than the life God has planned.

In horse training, my goal is always the perfect horse. I have never found the perfect horse, but when perfection is the goal, excellence is the result.

Settling for good enough will never get you good enough. Striving for perfection will always push you upward to amazing heights.

> *If your goal is to go the extra mile, prepare to pay an extra cost. Excellence is to be exceptional, surpassing, more competent and a step ahead with what is in your hands.* (Israelmore Ayivor)

Chapter 20

Slow Down

Danielle Crooks

Slow down and enjoy life. It's not only the scenery you miss by going too fast—you also miss the sense of where you are going and why.

—Eddie Cantor

In training inmates to train horses, I don't think it would be an exaggeration to say that I find myself saying "Slow down" a hundred times more often than "Speed up." Whether it is gentling a wild horse or training a domestic trail horse, the need to slow down is universally a challenge.

Training horses is a process that must focus on the mind, not the feet. That being the case, we must allow the horse to comprehend what we are asking, and comprehension is what takes time and patience.

Horses need to figure out what we are asking them to do. Since we speak a different language, we need to help them figure things out through slow, deliberate repetition. If we start slow, we give them the best chance to learn. If we start slow, we can add speed. If we start calm, we can add excitement. It rarely works the other way around.

The least resistance method of training horses is sometimes referred to as horse whispering. I think that label probably has more to do with the quietness of the trainer as he or she speaks softly to the horse. Speaking softly keeps the trainer calm and transfers to how we progress with the horse. Sometimes when working on a maneuver such as loping collected circles, I hum. I hum to calm myself and help the horse get into a rhythm. The interesting thing I have discovered is that over time the horse will hear the humming and automatically relax into a smoother gait.

I am not suggesting I want slow horses, but I do want relaxed horses. A horse thinks better when he is relaxed. Being relaxed is a mind-set not speed. A horse can be relaxed at a walk, trot, or lope. Conversely, a horse can be anxious standing still or at any gait. I slow down to give my horse the best chance to figure out what I am trying to teach and to help the horse relax.

Like horses, I make much better decisions when I am not in a hurry, anxious, stressed, or worried. In Shakespeare's classic *Romeo and Juliet*, Friar Lawrence gives young Romeo some great advice that would have changed the outcome of the tragedy. His advice to Romeo, "Go wisely and slowly. Those who rush stumble and fall."

God tells us in Psalm 46:10, "Be still, and know that I am God."

There are so many applications from horse training to life. Here are a few:

- If we start out fast, we will have difficulty getting energy down, which directly translates to safety and success.
- Thinking is always better than reacting. Those who act first and think later live lives of regret. An intentional life is not a reactive life filled with doing but a life focused on thought and purpose.
- Starting out slow begins with standing still. If a horse is moving when I am getting on, I know I have a horse that starts by acting, not thinking. I want a horse to stand still until I ask him to do something. Movement too often disconnects the mind.
- This is true for people. If we act before we think, we will find that we rarely learn and too often live with regret.
- It is easier to build movement and energy than to take it away. Slowing down does not mean we never speed up. Slowing down gives us the footing to move toward a goal and the energy to move quickly.

"I'm in a hurry to get things done, Oh, I rush and rush until life's no fun, All I really have to do live and die, But I'm in a hurry and don't know why," Alabama's 1992 hit song "I'm in a Hurry."

We need to slow down to get in touch with God. In the nineteenth chapter of 1 Kings, we find the prophet Elijah discouraged and drained. He desperately wanted to hear from God, so he ran a long distance to a cave.

While waiting securely in the cave for God to speak, he had a front-row seat to a display of tremendous power, energy, and excitement. The Bible tells us a strong hurricane force wind passed by, then there was an earthquake, followed by a fire. The Bible says that God was not in the wind, the earthquake, or the fire. After the fire died out and the dramatics ended, Elijah heard a whisper and knew it was God.

Pretty spectacular stuff! I would have concluded early on that God showed up, went out of the cave, and got blown off the side of the mountain. But Elijah knew a lot more about God than I do.

God was saying something profound to Elijah and, by inference, to you and me. Excitement, activity, and energy does not necessarily mean anything. God wanted Elijah to stand still, slow down, and listen.

I wonder how many times I've missed the supernatural by looking for the spectacular. I must admit that I am pretty impressed with hurricanes, earthquakes, and fire. But God wants me to listen for his still, small voice. He doesn't scream or throw things to get our attention. Instead, he whispers.

I have to remind myself of this when training a horse. I don't want to yank the horse's head around when I want him to turn. I want to pull the rein one inch to the right or to the left. I don't want to kick my horse to get him to move. I want to add the least amount of pressure to let the horse know I want him to move.

We must slow down if we are going to be able to hear what God is saying.

- Psalms 46:10, "*Be still and know that I am God.*"

  o Slow down your thoughts. Ask God to guide you to peace.

- 2 Corinthians 10:5, "*We take captive every thought to make it obedient to Christ.*"

  o Slow down before your thoughts have enough influence to become actions.

- James 1:19, "*You must all be quick to listen, slow to speak, and slow to get angry.*"

  o Slow down when you feel yourself getting angry.

- Proverbs 15:1, *"A soft answer turns away wrath, But a harsh word stirs up anger."*

  o Slow down before you say or do something you will regret

- Psalms 23:2, *"Lead me beside still waters."*

  o Ask God to give you peace and restore your soul.

Chapter 21

3 Second Ride

For a righteous man falls seven times, and rises again,
But the wicked stumble in time of disaster and
collapse.

— Proverbs 24:16, Amplified Bible

I sometimes wonder how certain sports got started. Bull riding would fit into that category. It probably started with a few cowboys on roundup daring one another to ride the meanest bull they had in the herd. Getting the bull captured would have been the first challenge, followed by getting the somewhat ill-advised cowboy on the bull's back. What followed was one mad bull, lots of dust, screams, bruises, and blood. When the dust settled, a cowboy emerged from the dirt and with a toothless grin said, "That was fun . . . Let's do it again, except this time with one hand in the air."

I was never a very good bull rider, but it is the only event I won a buckle in. The night I won the buckle is a much better memory than what happened the night before.

I was a police officer in Arlington, Texas, and a member of the Texas Police Officers Rodeo Association. That year the state rodeo was held in Mansfield, Texas, at the old Cow Bell Arena. Friday night was scheduled for practice, so I took my gear and headed to the arena to get a ride in. As cowboys do, I went to the back to get a look at the bulls. To me they seemed smaller than what I had ridden before, and for some reason I decided I really didn't need to do any stretches or prepare myself. This should be a piece of cake.

I drew a pretty nice practice bull, and he even seemed calm in the chute. The bull rope was cinched up tight, I nodded my head then raised my hand, and the gate swung open. That bull seemed to be equipped with small rocket launchers and exploded out of the chute while doing some pretty impressive midair twists. Suddenly I was on the ground only a few feet from the gate.

You wouldn't really think a person could reflect much about three seconds, but those few seconds can keep a guy from sleeping as the tape in your head replays over and over again in slow motion.

The person that makes excuses rarely makes changes.

I was raised to take responsibility for my actions, so I had to admit to myself that ego got in the way and I wasn't focused and prepared.

The next night I arrived at the rodeo with a lot more humility and a completely different attitude. I checked my gear, warmed up, did stretches, and mentally focused. I didn't know how the ride would end, but I knew I was as ready as I could be. There is nothing quite like hearing the eight-second buzzer when you are still riding.

The buckle usually stays in my closet, but when I see it hanging there, I am often reminded that I owe it all to a three-second ride.

Horses have taught me a lot about success, but the greatest lesson they have taught me is what to do when I have failed.

- Failure puts success in perspective.
- Failure lets us know what we don't want.
- Failure reminds us that winning it all and losing every-thing is separated by a fraction of a second or one mistake.
- The only people who fail are those who try, and trying is sometimes the most important thing.

Every failure brings us one step closer to success. Thomas Edison said, "Many of life's failures are people who did not realize how close they were to success when they gave up."

Most cowboys I know are, by nature, pretty humble. I think the main reason most cowboys possess humility is they have experienced failure but got up and kept working.

In life, we too often let failure define us. Failure will tell you what you are and tell you it is safer to stay where you are. The tragedy is not that we fail. The tragedy is when we conclude that we are a failure. Abraham Lincoln said, "My great concern is not whether you have failed, but whether you are content with your failure."

It is too easy to blame others or circumstances for our failures. It doesn't matter why. It only matters that we get up, brush ourselves off, and try again with newfound confidence and experience.

You can't go back and make a new start, but you can start right now and make a brand-new ending.

Chapter 22

. . . .

Never Give Up

And let us not grow weary while doing good, for in due season we shall reap if we do not lose heart.
Galatians 6:9

Successful people keep moving. They make mistakes, but they don't quit."
—Conrad Hilton

At some point in their career, every barrel racer will knock over a barrel, every roper will miss a steer, every bull rider will be thrown before 8 seconds, and every horse trainer will think to himself, "This is not going to work." Those who succeed are invariably those who have experienced failure, refused to be defined by failure, and never gave up.

Difficulties and setbacks are a normal part of working with horses. Every horse owner has been tempted to give up on trying to train a horse to do something, or they have decided that their particular horse is not able to change. I have been told by well-meaning horse owners that their horse is simply different from other horses and is not able to learn a task or routine. Rarely is that true.

Once we conclude "My horse is different," we start making excuses and quit trying to train. The end result is we rob the horse of the opportunity to reach his potential. We don't think of it as quitting at first. Instead we think of it as trying something different to see if another method will work. But the horse doesn't see it this way. For the horse, we quit one thing that he was trying to figure out and introduced another thing that he has try to figure out. Each time, our horse is more confused and our job is more difficult. If we stick with what we are doing, we give the horse the best possible opportunity to figure it out.

I've lost count of how many times I've watched well-intentioned horse owners try to load a horse that refuses to get in the trailer. Usually the episode begins with one person inside the trailer urgently pulling on the lead rope of a reluctant horse. When that doesn't work, they bribe the horse with hay or grain. They soon resort back to pulling, this time with more force. A crowd forms, and a couple people flail their arms or hats in an attempt to scare the horse forward. Eventually in desperation, someone places a rope over the horse's butt, and then on the count of three, two people pull on the butt, another pulls on the lead, and everyone else frantically waves blankets hats and arms yelling as though they were on a cattle drive.

Think about it from the perspective of the poor horse. It began with the fact that he was afraid or unsure about going into this metal cave on wheels. As soon as he said he didn't want to go, the pressure increased. He insisted on not going in the trailer, so the pressure stopped, and someone gave him hay. For some reason, he won that battle, and now someone was rewarding him. Now the same pressure was reapplied, so he did the same thing he was rewarded for before. As far as he knew, at that point, his job was to pull back so someone would give him a treat. Now, however, people started trying to scare him, then a rope was placed around his butt, then more people flailing their arms. The purpose in the horse's mind was now totally lost. He just wanted to avoid that place where all the craziness, fear, and pressure took place, which unfortunately was the entrance to the trailer.

The horse was never allowed to make a choice. In a short period of time, these people gave up on a number of things they were doing, so the horse's frustration increased.

By saying "Never give up," I mean never give up on what you believe will work and what you believe will help the horse calmly figure out what you want.

One of my favorite horses was a gelding named Major. He was a beautiful red roan that I used when I first started doing horsemanship clinics. Sometimes Major took a little longer to figure things out. There were times when I thought, "He is not going to get it." However, as I kept working with him, I found that he not only got it, but once he did, it was locked in. I had to stay consistent and allow him to figure things out.

Bear Bryant was one of the most famous college football coaches in history. When he retired, he had led the University of Alabama to 6 National championships and 323 wins, and at that time he held the record as the most winning coach in history. Bear Bryant's philosophy was, *"Never quit. Set a goal and don't quit until you attain it. When you do attain it, set another goal, and don't quit until you reach it. Never quit."*

Whether training a horse, coaching a football team, or trying to succeed in life, the principle doesn't change. Refuse to quit.

Just like horse owners who conclude their horse is unique and not able to succeed, there are people who conclude that their life, failures, and circumstances are so unique it is impossible to succeed and they quit. How many battles have been won in the eleventh hour? How many basketball games have been won seconds before the buzzer? How many horses have come from the backstretch and won the race? How many people have refused to quit to find that victory was waiting in the next step?

Life is much more important than basketball games and horse races, yet too often we quit in the eleventh hour or entering the home stretch.

Therefore, since we have so great a cloud of witnesses surrounding us, let us also lay aside every encumbrance and the sin which so easily entangles us, and let us run with endurance the race that is set before us, fixing our eyes on Jesus, the author and perfecter of faith, who for the joy set before Him endured the cross, despising the shame, and has sat down at the right hand of the throne of God. (Hebrews 12:1–2)

Chapter 23

The Edge of a Precipice

Examine me, O Lord, and try me; Test my mind and my heart.

— Psalm 26:2

There is an old Spanish proverb that says, "Never train a horse on the edge of a precipice." Find out what you are made of before your actions can damage yourself or others.

Descending for 4,460 feet for almost 8 miles on a steep trail that winds through narrow passages, tunnels, and a 25- to 30-degree drop in temperature is quite an accomplishment. Add to that weather changes, hikers, wild animals, and an occasional bicycle, and you have defined the trail into the Grand Canyon.

Imagine riding a mule down the zigzagging canyon trail on a beautiful crisp morning. You look over the edge to catch a glimpse of the Colorado River winding thousands of feet below. Overhead you see a bald eagle catching the updrafts and look down in time to notice a deer effortlessly jumping from one rocky ledge to another before descending out of sight. A cool breeze is blowing filling the air with the relaxing smell of pine trees. Your serenity is interrupted by a question from the old weather-beaten guide. "How's your mule comin' along?" he asks. "Fine, I think," only to hear the concerning response, "Good, he's greenbroke and has never been on the trail before".

Your prayer life just took on a different intensity, and what began as a peaceful ride has become an anxiety filled adventure with dread and a sense of panic each time the mule seems to stumble or gets too close to edge. You don't dare look up and forget watching for animals. The priority has shifted to survival.

The old Spanish proverb seemed to capture this idea: "*Never train a horse on the edge of a precipice.*" Don't wait until you are in the midst of a crisis before at least having an idea of what you should do.

Before a horse or mule makes a trip into the Grand Canyon, they are thoroughly evaluated, trained, and tested. Before they ever make a trip down the trail, they are exposed to bicyclists, hikers, encounters with animals, and weather conditions. There are predictable hazards like wind, rain, bicyclists, and small animals. The predictable dangers are more easily trained for. By far the most dangerous are the unexpected encounters, like rude people coming up the other way, blowing debris, and sounds. Because of this, the horses and mules make the trip numerous times before they have acquired enough experience to carry a pack or a rider. The trail can be a dangerous place, and it only takes one bad decision or misstep for the expedition to end in tragedy.

Horses need repetition and testing to develop confidence and security. They must go through a process to develop the tools necessary to succeed. The trip is the fun part. The process is often tedious.

I don't like instructions and owner's manuals. I confess, if I buy something that needs assembly, the first thing I do is try to figure it out without reading the instructions. Sometimes this works with furniture and cars, but in life it can destroy us. God gave us the Bible as a manual to equip us for the journey ahead. In 2 Timothy 3:16, it says, *"All Scripture is inspired by God and is useful to teach us what is true and to make us realize what is wrong in our lives. It corrects us when we are wrong and teaches us to do what is right"* (NLT).

I train horses to do a lot of things that seem to have no practical application. Sometimes they look at me as if to say, "Why are we doing this?" They will walk over a tarp, stand on a pedestal, sit on a beanbag chair, walk over a teetering bridge, allow a ten-foot tarp to be draped over their entire body, wear the saddle hanging from their side, and the list could go on. I do what I can to put their mind and emotions to the test.

I remember the first time I took my horse inside a building filled with people for a cowboy church. We were privileged to be at a men's retreat called Man Camp in Prescott, Arizona. The first service was inside the main auditorium with spotlights, a sound system, and four hundred excited men. Starbuck had never been in a situation quite like that, so before the retreat, I took him inside my garage, a wedding chapel, and a church. I did my best to help him understand how to respond in an unfamiliar situation.

He didn't have any idea why we were going inside buildings, but he took it all in stride as he learned to adjust to the lights and sounds. For horses, understanding the why is not important. They just need to know what is expected, how they are going to do it, and that it will not hurt them.

I can't say he enjoyed being in an auditorium filled with people, but I knew he was tested and ready.

Jeremiah 29:11 (NKJV) says, *"For I know the thoughts that I think toward you, says the LORD, thoughts of peace and not of evil, to give you a future and a hope."*

Most people go to great lengths to avoid something they deem unpleasant or unnecessary. We avoid them even more when they do not seem to make sense. The edge of a precipice (side of a cliff) is not the place to train a horse, and the middle of a crisis is not the best place to start looking for answers. Life is filled with dangers, difficulties, and things we do not understand. We need to learn to welcome opportunities to be prepared for the unexpected.

God tells the prophet Habakkuk, *"I am doing something in your own day, something you wouldn't believe even if someone told you about it"* (Habakkuk 1:5). Just because something is difficult or we do not understand, it does not mean that it is not part of God's plan to prepare us for what lies ahead.

I certainly don't enjoy the tests that show up in my life, but I have grown to appreciate them. The more often I get hurt or hurt others, the more I understand the importance of tests.

In life, we often suffer loss because we are we not prepared for the trail we are on. We too often think we will cross that bridge when we come to it and miss the opportunities to prepare for the bridge.

I look at obstacle courses, arenas, and training routines like boot camp for horses. In training horses, I have a seven-acre training course where I developed obstacles and routines. Each obstacle is something that any horse can safely do. However, it pushes the horse to grow and learn. Each obstacle is designed to prepare a horse to face uncomfortable situations with confidence. Every routine is developed to challenge the horse to grow. Many of the obstacles are things that horse will probably never encounter. I don't anticipate coming across brightly colored pedestals, teetering bridges, or tunnels made of huge tires while on the trail. However, I do anticipate washes, boulders, terrain and canyons.

What obstacles are you avoiding that could prepare you for the journey ahead?

Search me, O God, and know my heart; Try me and know my anxious thoughts. (Psalm 139:23)

Chapter 24

When Training Ends

I have fought the good fight, I have finished the course, I have kept the faith.
—2 Timothy 4:7

Spiritual growth has a lot of parallels to horses and horse training.

Horses change from being untouchable to being amazing partners. They progress from resisting pressure to yielding to pressure. A horse accomplishes hundreds of things throughout his training.

Throughout life, we encounter an incredible amount of information and experiences. We have learned thousands of new things.

We have little idea what the future holds, but if the past is an indication, we know that there is more to learn, more to experience, and more to overcome before we cross the finish line.

The good news is that if you and I stay consistent and continue to grow, eventually we will cross the finish line.

Does training ever really end? There is a significant difference between finish lines and *the* finish line. In clinics I will occasionally ask, "When are you finished training your horse?" The answer should be, "When the horse dies or I do." Horse training is a lifelong commitment to grow and improve.

I enjoy watching competitors prepare their horses for events. They work on timing, speed, and control. Rarely do you see a serious competitor drive up, get the horse out of trailer, and immediately compete. They fine-tune themselves and their horse as they get prepared for what is ahead. Even the best horses need continual tuning up. Horses that compete on the pro circuit never stop training.

The very fact that there is a finish line should compel us to continue moving toward the goal. The more you live, the more you learn, and the more you learn, the more you realize how little you know.

In the wild horse inmate program, we have hundreds of horses to select from. These horses are kept in large pens and cared for by inmates. Once a wild horse reaches six or seven years old, it is generally deemed too old to start training. This number of older horses included some amazing horses that were not even considered. I decided to see what would happen if we brought a few of the older horses over to training. We began the experiment with a beautiful eleven-year-old grulla gelding. He was phenomenal and changed our process of selecting horses. In a short period of time, this horse that was considered too old surpassed most of the other horses. We named him Dozer because he would plow through any obstacle or situation. He turned out to be an amazing horse and was adopted to work on a remote cattle ranch in central Arizona. Dozer quickly became one of the ranch foreman's favorite horses.

If we hadn't decided to give him a chance, Dozer would have lived out the rest of his life in a large pen with food, shade, and water. Instead, he was given a new purpose and destiny beyond his wildest dreams. We can learn a lot from this eleven-year-old wild horse that was willing to be trained and accept an entirely different life than anything he knew.

Multitudes of wonderful people are convinced that their best days are behind them. Setbacks, limitations, age, or the past have somehow been allowed to declare that they just need to settle. When we settle, we stop growing, and without even realizing it, we refuse to learn.

Training horses reminds me that I can change. They help me realize how much better I can be, how much more I can learn.

When does training end for you and me? The answer for us is the same answer for horses: when we die. As long as you are breathing, you have purpose, and as long as you have purpose, you need to grow.

I was fifty-seven years old when I was certified as a horse trainer and fifty-eight years old when I was hired as the wild horse and burro inmate supervisor for the state prison. When I should have been thinking about enjoying retirement, I was embarking on a new adventure. I still have a lot to learn and learning has become a passion.

It doesn't matter how many years you have lived or attended church or how many scriptures you memorize or songs you can sing. Spiritual growth is all about willingness to change and be stretched. Spiritual growth and maturity is not about fixing our eyes on the finish line but fixing our eyes on the Author and Finisher of our faith as we continue to run the race that he set before us.

When does training end? As long as you are breathing.

Therefore, since we have so great a cloud of witnesses surrounding us, let us also lay aside every encumbrance and the sin which so easily entangles us, and let us run with endurance the race that is set before us, looking unto Jesus, the author and finisher of our faith . . . (Hebrews 12:1–2)

About the Author

Randy was born into a ranching and farming family in central Arizona. After four years in the United States Air Force, he served as an undercover narcotics officer, patrolman, and chaplain in Texas and Arizona. After serving as a pastor for over thirty years, he was offered the position to develop and supervise the Arizona Wild Horse Inmate Program, where he trains inmates and wild horses for the Arizona Department of Corrections.

The program has had a remarkable effect in not only training wild horses but also transforming the lives of inmates. The success of the wild horse inmate program has been the subject of local, national, and international news stories and documentaries including *Animal Planet*, ABC, NBC *Nightly News*, and *USA Today*. Randy is a Lyons Legacy–certified horse trainer and travels extensively conducting horse training clinics, cowboy churches, and ministry to men.